❧ TEA & COOKIES ❧

ALSO BY RICK RODGERS

The Turkey Cookbook

365 Ways to Cook Hamburger and Other Ground Meats

Mr. Pasta's Healthy Pasta Cookbook

Fondue

Slow Cooker Ready & Waiting

The Baker's Dozen Cookbook (ed.)

Dip It

Thanksgiving 101

Christmas 101

Summer Gatherings

Autumn Gatherings

Winter Gatherings

Spring Gatherings

Coffee and Cake

Kaffeehaus

TEA & COOKIES

Enjoy the Perfect
Cup of Tea—with Dozens
of Delectable Recipes
for Teatime Treats

RICK RODGERS

PHOTOGRAPHS BY BEN FINK

WILLIAM MORROW
An Imprint of HarperCollinsPublishers

HarperCollins books may be purchased for educational, business, or sales promotional use. For information please write: Special Markets Department, HarperCollins Publishers, 10 East 53rd Street, New York, NY 10022.

FIRST EDITION

Designed by Lorie Pagnozzi

Library of Congress Cataloging-in-Publication Data
Rodgers, Rick, 1953–
    Tea and cookies : enjoy the perfect cup of tea—with dozens of delectable recipes for teatime treats / Rick Rodgers ; photographs by Ben Fink.—1st ed.
        p. cm.
    Includes index.
    ISBN 978-0-06-193833-7
1. Afternoon teas. 2. Tea. 3. Cookies. I. Title.
    TX736.R64 2010
    642—dc22

                                                            2009044021

---

10 11 12 13 14   OV/RRD   10 9 8 7 6 5 4 3 2 1

ACKNOWLEDGMENTS

This journey with tea and cookies has been delicious and edifying in equal parts. I was lucky to have had personal tastings with three major forces in the tea world: Adrienne Etkin of Admari Tea, Michael Harney of Harney and Sons, and Miriam Novelle of T Salon. Each expert enlightened me in his or her own way to the nuances of tea. Adrienne spontaneously served me my first properly brewed white tea, served in consecutive steepings in tiny cups. Michael did a full presentation of many teas at a local tea shop, Tea Time in Short Hills, New Jersey, that inspired and educated everyone there. And Miriam gave me a guide of her specialty, blended teas.

Thanks to David Sweeney for supporting the concept of this book and its companion, *Coffee and Cakes*. It is always a pleasure to be edited by Cassie Jones, whose personal grace shines through in her work. Jessica Deputato, Cassie's assistant, brings her own impressive skills to the table. Sonia Greenbaum was the ever-helpful copy editor, who stopped me from spelling pu-erh three different ways. I have design director Lorie Pagnozzi to thank for the visual appeal of the book, and Adam Rochkind and Dee Dee DeBartlo for the publicity side of things.

Once again, Ben Fink provided gorgeous photos. Food photography is hard work, but we always have a good time in spite of the long days. Special thanks to my friends and neighbors Skip Dye and Steven King for letting me raid their collection of extraordinary antique teapots, teacups, cake plates, and more. My longtime assistant, Diane Kniss, kept the whole operation afloat with her customary good cheer. A tea lover herself, my agent, Susan Ginsburg, was her usual guiding light, and her assistant, Bethany Stout, always took my phone calls and solved innumerable problems. All of these people are not just colleagues but invaluable and beloved friends. And Patrick Fisher cheered us all on from the sidelines.

CONTENTS

The classic Japanese tea ceremony.

INTRODUCTION

For centuries, tea has been served whenever people gather. In Japan, where tea is deeply rooted in the culture, a tea ceremony is one of the highest honors that a host can bestow on his guests. Chinese culture also reveres tea, and at a traditional wedding, the bride and groom serve their parents tea as a symbol of their respect and devotion. In many

Russian homes, the samovar, a gorgeous metal urn for holding brewed tea, is prominently displayed as the family's primary heirloom. And while the meal known as British High Tea began as a way to feed the upper classes, it can also be informal, and at its finest is a time for serving beautifully prepared edibles on your best china.

This sensibility has carried over to America, where an invitation to take tea promises more than just a meal; it is an opportunity for intimate conversation and peaceful reflection. In my corner of New Jersey, I have three world-class tea purveyors within a short drive of my house, and a number of appropriately cozy tea shops offering tea parties.

But what should accompany a cup of tea? While savory foods are usually on the menu, sweets are a constant. When food is carefully prepared in bite-size portions, the elegance factor rises. And cookies, which are really just small, individually sized cakes, are always part of the teatime menu.

Tea and Cookies celebrates this happy combination of beverage and dessert. The book starts with a primer on the basics of tea, from production to pouring the perfect cup. It is followed by a collection of hot and cold tea-based beverages that demonstrate unique ways to enjoy your cup.

After another primer on the important elements of baking cookies (ingredients, equipment, and techniques), you'll find sweet things to nibble on, inspired by tea-friendly foods from all over the globe—from French madeleines and *macarons* to Scottish shortbread. Some of the cookies are particularly sophisticated (such as the dramatically dark Chocolate Sandwich Cookies with Earl Grey Ganache), but even the rustic or homey varieties have a twist that will take them beyond mere snack foods (the Snickerdoodles are flavored with spices that you are likely to find in Indian chai).

Whether you are serving a large group of friends, preparing a quiet tea for two, or indulging in a personal treat, this book will guide you through the perfect pairings of tea and cookies.

A TEA PRIMER

After water, tea is the most consumed beverage in the world. Entire books have been devoted to its history, production, and cultural role, to name just a few topics. While by no means exhaustive, this primer serves as an introduction to tea that will help you make an informed purchase at any tea shop.

HISTORY OF TEA ❧

The story of tea begins in the mountainous area where present-day China, Vietnam, Myanmar, and Thailand meet, but it was the far-reaching Chinese culture that helped bring this ancient delicacy to all corners of the world. In today's languages, almost every word for tea has evolved from the Cantonese and Mandarin (*cha*) or Amoy dialect (*te*).

For at least three thousand years, humans have brewed the leaves of the evergreen *Camellia sinensis* tea bush. One legend of tea's origin tells how the Divine Farmer saw some leaves from a nearby tree fall into a pot of boiling water. His curiosity drew him to taste the brew, and tea was discovered.

In ancient China, tea was regarded not only as a food, but as a medicine. The three main religions of China—Buddhism, Confucianism, and Taoism—all considered tea to be a source of health and rejuvenation (monks noticed that it would keep them alert during meditation). From its origins, tea was regarded as more than just a way to quench one's thirst. But the technique of steeping tea leaves in hot water and then pouring the liquid into cups didn't evolve until the Chinese Ming era (1368–1644).

By the ninth century, tea consumption had spread to Japan, probably when Buddhist monks brought home tea seeds from a pilgrimage to China. The Japanese picked up some of the rituals surrounding tea from the Chinese court, and these developed into the graceful tea ceremony that is still performed today. Japanese drinkers developed a preference for green tea, which is minimally processed, while the Chinese produced more complex, oxidized black tea along with the green tea varieties.

Tea was not introduced to Europe until the mid-seventeenth century. It was the Portuguese, then a major naval power, who first came upon tea during trade with China. Holland was politically affiliated with Portugal at the time, and tea became popular in The Hague. The British had their first brush with tea when Charles II married the Portuguese Infanta, Catherine of Braganza, and she introduced the Chinese beverage and its elegant serving rituals to the court. Here tea repeated the same modus operandi it had in Portugal and Holland, beginning as an expensive drink for the upper class but evolving into a beverage for common citizens as trade routes improved and prices plummeted. Before long, Parliament established monopolies to control the tea as a commodity, a policy that turned out to make lots of trouble for Britain around the world over the centuries.

As for America, New Amsterdam (later New York) was a Dutch colony well acquainted with the pleasures of tea, so it surfaced early in our country's history. Among other indignities, it was the British manipulation of tea prices that led to the infamous Boston Tea Party and the start of the American Revolution.

While tea was an important beverage in British life, it reached its peak in the early 1800s, when it became the centerpiece of a light afternoon meal. At the time, there were only two meals, breakfast and dinner. Anna, the seventh Duchess of Bedford, started offering a light repast in the late afternoon to tide over the appetites of her entourage at her summer castle. It was such a success that when she returned to London, she kept up the practice. This started a fashion for afternoon tea, which emphasized genteel conversation without alcoholic beverages. Before tea, gin and beer were the most popular British beverages, and the cause of many social problems.

Throughout the eighteenth century, the British coffeehouses served both coffee (another tropical delicacy) and tea, and were social gathering places that were essentially men's clubs. In the early nineteenth century, tea gardens, outgrowths of coffeehouses, became especially popular because they allowed (accompanied) middle-class women as clientele. (The first tea garden was owned by Thomas Twining, whose tea company is still a major force in the industry.) To get immediate attention from the waiter, a gentleman was invited to put money in a box marked "T. I. P. S.," an acronym for To Insure Prompt Service, and the beginning of our custom of giving gratuities to restaurant servers.

Tea, which grows in tropical and subtropical conditions, was not the only reason for British colonization in hot climates, but the practice did help keep Britain well supplied with this important commodity. British efforts made India the most important region for tea production in the world. In the mid-1800s, after much experimentation with different varieties, a hybrid of Chinese and the local Assam tea (which may or may not be a strain of the Chinese plant) was developed, creating a particularly vigorous plant that became the backbone of the international tea industry. Indian tea remains a force because it is a primary ingredient in many of the most popular blended teas, especially supermarket varieties.

Two important American innovations changed the way people drink tea: iced tea and the tea bag. The first was the result of a vendor's effort at the 1904 St. Louis World's Fair to unload some hot tea that wasn't selling well in the oppressive summer weather—poured over ice, the tea was a hit. Tea bags were originally small paper packages of loose tea that were used by a tea merchant as samples. He noticed that his customers were not removing the tea from the bags to save them the trouble of straining out the leaves, and tea bags were born. Tea bags were a great timesaver, as tea could be made right in the cup without a teapot and strainer, but they also diminished the role of ritual in making tea.

In recent years, the romance of tea has returned with a renewed interest in fine teas sold by boutique tea merchants, mirroring the consumer's interest in better coffee and wine. Teas with the flavors of spices, herbs, and fruits have brought new audiences to this ancient drink. Tearooms, many serving afternoon tea meals, are now vying with coffee bars as community gathering places.

TYPES OF TEA ❧

The production of tea is similar to wine, as the soil, climate, time of harvest, handling, processing, and other factors all contribute to the quality of the final product. All tea is produced from the leaves (and sometimes buds) of a single evergreen plant related to the magnolia, *Camellia sinensis*. It is how the leaves are processed after picking that gives the tea its color and main flavor characteristics.

Freshly picked tea leaves.

When tea leaves are picked, they will eventually change color, the same way that cut fruit darkens when exposed to oxygen. Controlling the extent of oxidation, along with fermenting, rolling, crushing, and drying the leaves, are all ways to vary the flavor of tea leaves. Another important factor is when the tea leaves are harvested. The growth of shoots on the tea plant is called a "flush." The first flush, considered the best for varieties such as Darjeeling, occurs in the spring, when only the youngest leaves are harvested. The subsequent second (summer) and third (late summer or autumn) flushes yield stronger leaves with harsher flavors.

There are five major categories of tea. In order of complexity of processing (which generally translates into depth of flavor), they are white, green, oolong, black, and pu-erh. Within these groups are presentation teas, blends, and flavored teas. Although the term "herbal tea" is commonly used to describe a beverage made from the leaves, bark, root, flowers, or twigs of plants, this is incorrect, as only beverages made from *Camellia sinensis* leaves are truly tea. I have included them because most people don't make the distinction.

Here are brief explanations of each kind of tea, with some of my personal favorites that are representative of the particular style.

WHITE TEA

The least processed of the five major teas, white tea contains the youngest leaf tips and buds of tea plants. Unlike other teas, which are heated or oxidized, the fuzzy tea leaves are only air-dried, which retains the silvery white "down" that gives the tea its name.

Originally a specialty of the Fujian province of China, white tea is now harvested as well in other tea-producing regions, such as Darjeeling and Assam. These teas are always served plain in order to savor the very delicate and subtle flavor. Some white tea, known as artisan or presentation tea, is processed for visual appeal—the dried buds are tied together with osmanthus or other blossoms to create a bouquet that will unfurl in hot water. In order to see the transformation, brew this tea in a glass pot. White tea is often prepared in a series of short infusions, allowing the flavor to develop slowly.

Top left, **Silver Needles**; *bottom right,* **Pomegranate Bai Mu Dan.**

Brewed Inner Blossom Osmanthus,
an artisan-style white tea.

Silver Needles, from Fujian, has long, thin, curled leaves that retain their silvery-white fuzzy surface, and is the top grade of Chinese white tea.

Bai Mu Dan, the second grade of Chinese white tea, is also known as White Peony.

GREEN TEA

The leaves for green tea are never oxidized, so the vegetal, even grassy flavor is very close to the original leaf. First, the leaves are steamed to halt oxidation and set the verdant color, then they are rolled, spread out, and dried by more applied heat. Japan uses a hot-air process that ensures a delicate flavor. However, in China the leaves are often heated on a hot surface in a process called "firing," curling the leaves into an elongated shape and giving the brewed tea a deeper richness. The processing of green tea, from steaming to the final drying, takes only about three hours. Green tea can be sweetened, but it should not be served with milk.

Clockwise from top left: **Dragonwell, Matcha, Genmaicha, Sencha.**

Chinese Green Tea

Green tea accounts for about two-thirds of Chinese tea production, and is often graded according to time of harvest, similar to the flush system. The First Spring crop collects only the plant buds in April; Second Spring includes some leaves in early June; and Third Spring harvests in July, but most of the flavor has been depleted, so the tea is used for mass-market consumption. Some Chinese green teas:

DRAGONWELL is visually identified by its long, wide leaves, which are kept intact by careful hand-firing. One of the classic Chinese teas, and a favorite of the emperors, it is still served at special occasions—it is the tea that Mao Tse-tung offered to Richard Nixon. Dragonwell is named for the town of its origin (Longjing, or Lung Ching in Chinese), which legend says had a water spring that was home to a dragon.

GUNPOWDER also has a distinctive shape, its leaves hand-rolled into pellets that resemble military gunpowder. Its fairly strong flavor makes it a good green tea to try if you are a black tea fan. Much of the gunpowder tea production is shipped to the Middle East and Morocco, where it is often brewed with peppermint.

GREEN SNAIL is sometimes sold by its Chinese name, Bi Lo Chun. Only the first two leaves and buds are hand-picked during the First Spring harvest, and, when dried, they take on the curly snail shape that gives the tea its name.

Japanese Green Tea

So much green tea is consumed in Japan that only 2 percent of the product is exported. The famous tea ceremony (*chanoyu*), a ritualized presentation and serving of matcha tea, was refined and popularized sometime in the fifteenth century by Murata Juko, the Zen priest who is considered the first Tea Master. Today, the intricacies of this tranquil ceremony are still studied and practiced not just in Japan, but by its admirers all over the world. The following list names some Japanese green teas that you are likely to find at a well-stocked tea shop.

SENCHA is the most common Japanese green tea, made from the first and second flushes. It is known as "broiled" tea because the tea plants are grown in full sunlight. My local tea shop makes a big fuss over the arrival of their shipment of the very first picking, *shincha*.

BANCHA is grown from the same plant as sencha, but the third and fourth flushes are used instead. The late harvesting lowers its quality, but also its price, making it the everyday tea for many green tea drinkers.

GENMAICHA is sencha that has been flavored with puffed brown rice kernels, giving the tea a popcornlike aroma and mild nutty flavor. Many Japanese restaurants serve genmaicha to accompany their food.

GYOKURO, the highest grade of Japanese tea, starts out as sencha, grown in full sunlight. But two weeks before the harvest, the plants are covered and protected from light, which changes their flavor while it increases their caffeine content. Gyokuro requires a special brewing method—use water only heated to about 140°F, and steep the leaves for about 90 seconds. Because the tea will not be piping hot, be sure to warm the teapot and cups with hot water before brewing and serving. Its name translates to "Jade Dew," which refers to the light green color of the brewed tea.

HOJICHA, "roasted tea," is bancha (or sometimes sencha) leaves heated in a porcelain pot over charcoal, which gives it a roasted flavor. This process also naturally removes some of the caffeine, which is why some people choose hojicha as their bedtime tea.

MATCHA, green tea leaves ground into a talclike fluorescent green powder, is used in the *chanoyu* ceremony, where it is whipped with hot water into a froth with a special bamboo whisk. Matcha can also be added to desserts (especially ice cream and custards) and some savory dishes (such as soba noodles) as a flavoring and coloring.

OOLONG TEA

The leaves for oolong tea are partially oxidized, giving the brew a flavor that has some of the bite of black tea, while retaining a bit of the grassiness of green tea. The amount of oxidation, from 10 to 80 percent, is determined by the producer. Oxidation also brings out the tea's fruity notes, evident in the aroma of brewed oolong tea. The leaves can be long and curled, or rolled into pellets.

Top left, **Formosa Milk;** *bottom right,* **Phoenix Dan Cong.**

The most famous Chinese oolongs are from the high elevations around Wuyi Mountain in the Fujian province, but Taiwan is also known for its oolong, and some Indians give their Darjeeling the oolong treatment.

Unlike many other teas, which become bitter if brewed too long, oolong tea improves with multiple brewings. The first two steepings are mild, but the flavor increases and blooms with the third and fourth steepings. The best way to enjoy oolong's nuances is without sugar or milk. The following list identifies a variety of oolong teas:

DA HONG PAO (Big Red Robe or Royal Red Robe) is one of the most famous oolong teas from Fujian province. Its very large leaves are highly oxidized to give the tea a mild astringency similar to black tea.

IRON GODDESS (Tie Guan Yin in Chinese) is probably named for an iron statue of the goddess of compassion. It is not very heavily oxidized, and has a light color and flavor. If designated "monkey-picked," that does not mean that it was literally harvested by chimpanzees. There is a legend that Buddhist monks trained monkeys to pick the youngest leaves from plants growing on cliffs that were inaccessible to humans, but today the term means that only the most delicate leaves were used to produce the tea.

PHOENIX DAN CONG hails from the area around Phoenix Mountain in the Quangdong region of China. *Dan cong* means "single bush," a highly regarded strain of tea plant that has been cultivated for more than seven hundred years. Quangdong teas have very distinctive fruit and floral aromas, such as melon, peach, and magnolia.

FORMOSA MILK, from Taiwan, has a surprising milky aroma and buttery mouth feel. These attributes are the result of a sudden climate change that occurs during the plant's growth.

BLACK TEA

Black tea leaves are allowed to oxidize to the fullest, a process that includes wilting, rolling, and drying. This combination of treatments deepens the tea's flavor and darkens its brewed color. Although the other teas are increasing in popularity, black tea accounts for over 90 percent of sales in the West. Unblended black tea is often identified by its place of origin. Different kinds of black tea can be combined to create blends, or mixed with flavorings.

Brewed black tea actually has a reddish color—in fact, it is called "red tea" in China. (In the West, red tea refers to rooibos, which is not a tea at all.) The term "black tea" probably refers to the very dark tea leaves.

As tea leaves can be crushed and broken during processing, leaf size is the main quality indicator for black tea. The best class is whole-leaf tea, which indicates careful handling. Orange Pekoe is not a specific kind of tea, but a size of tea leaf. (The "Orange" in the term probably is a nod to the royal family of Orange, who were in power when the British tea trade was becoming a major commercial force, and has nothing to do with citrus flavor.) You may find some teas labeled with an acronym such as TGFOP (Tippy Golden Flowery Orange Pekoe), an even more specific grade, which in this case denotes that, along with the leaves, the tea includes the desirable golden tips and flowers of the tea branches.

Broken leaves can be sold as a less expensive, but still good-quality tea. Fannings (small pieces of leaves left over from processing larger-leaf teas) and dust (even smaller particles of leaves) end up in tea bags. Small-leaf particles have harsher flavors.

Clockwise from top left: **Jasmine, Golden Monkey, Black Snail, Lapsang Souchong.**

This is one reason why tea bags, which have traditionally been filled with fannings and dust, have a bad reputation among tea connoisseurs. On the other hand, the small pieces have more surface area to come into contact with hot water, and thus release their flavor quickly for a fast cup of tea. The commonplace black teas are often sweetened and doused with milk to help soften the rough flavor, but high-quality black tea can be savored plain. Here are some familiar black teas:

Chinese Black Tea

KEEMUN, named for its place of origin in Qimen (Keemun being its colonial period spelling) county in eastern China, is full-bodied and strong when brewed, with aromas of pine and fruit. Its strength made it a popular tea for blending, but now it is appreciated as a single-leaf tea.

YUNNAN, from the traditional birthplace of Chinese tea, is malty with spicy notes. YUNNAN GOLD tea includes the golden tips of the plant buds; pricey YUNNAN PURE GOLD is composed exclusively of these carefully harvested buds.

SNAIL tea is made from leaves that have been hand-curled into tight spirals; GOLDEN SNAIL tea includes a high amount of leafy tips. The curly leaves unfurl slowly in hot water, making this one of the few black teas that can take to two or three consecutive brewings, similar to the method used for some white teas.

GOLDEN MONKEY, from the Fujian province, is hand-plucked to include only one leaf and one bud. The dried leaves, with golden highlights, are said to resemble a monkey's claws.

Indian Tea

DARJEELING tea is processed from small-leaved Chinese tea plants planted in this region of West Bengal in the mid-1800s by the British. The best Darjeeling comes from small plantations called tea gardens, many of them with romantic names such as Margaret's Hope or Happy Valley, and identified by the time of their harvest (first flush through autumn). The brewed tea is light-bodied with a winelike aroma that reminds many of muscatel.

ASSAM tea is made from large-leaved tea plants native to India. The dried leaves are sizable and twisted, and brew into a reddish-brown beverage with the slightly astringent "brisk" flavor that makes it a fine morning eye-opener.

CEYLON, the colonial name of the island Sri Lanka, grows tea in six different regions. For a variety with the classic black tea "brightness" of flavor, look for one from the Central Highlands region. Sri Lanka is the third-largest producer of tea in the world.

Blended Black Tea

ENGLISH BREAKFAST tea blends various Indian black teas to make a robust flavor that does well with milk and sugar.

IRISH BREAKFAST tea is even stronger than its English counterpart, and usually has a base of Assam tea. To mellow its assertiveness, it is usually drunk with milk and sugar.

RUSSIAN CARAVAN tea mixes very strong black tea with Lapsang Souchong to give the brew a smoky aroma reminiscent of a caravan campfire. Russians love tea, which is brewed very strong, then diluted (preferably with water from the family samovar, which is heated all day to stand at the ready), and served highly sweetened with sugar or jam.

EARL GREY tea is a blend of black teas processed with oil of the bergamot orange to give it a unique fragrance and flavor. It is named for the British prime minister of the 1830s.

Flavored Teas

Many popular teas are flavored with fruit or spices—currant, peach, blueberry, cinnamon, and orange are just a few of the ingredients that you will see on tea labels. To provide the flavor, the tea leaves (usually black) are often sprayed with natural or artificial oils. In some cases, the leaves are mixed with dried peels or spices or dehydrated fruit. JASMINE, one of the best-known flavored teas, is green or black tea stored with actual jasmine blossoms to absorb the flowers' strong scent and mild flavor. LAPSANG SOUCHONG is black tea that has been smoked over pine to give it a very smoky flavor.

PU-ERH TEAS

Fermentation and aging after oxidation both contribute to pu-erh tea's woodsy flavor and aroma. The large leaves are from a wild tea tree that grows in the Yunnan province. There are actually two types of pu-erh. Green (also called "raw") pu-erh is unoxidized, then fermented to give it a particularly earthy flavor. "Cooked" pu-erh has been lightly oxidized, and is then fermented before being pressed into various shapes (such as disks, nests, bowls, mushrooms, squares, or bricks) that can be aged for years. These molded, compact shapes made the tea easier to transport by horse. Today, the molds are often wrapped in paper for selling. To brew pu-erh, the leaf is chipped off the mold and then steeped in water.

Top, **Seven Sisters;** *bottom,* **Tuo Cha.**

Even though cooked pu-erh is essentially an oolong tea, it turns black during aging, so the Chinese refer to it as "black tea." Pu-erh tea is said to have extraordinary health properties, and it is renowned in China as a diet tea.

Tuo Cha is pu-erh tea pressed into a bird's-nest or bowl shape. The molded tea bowl can be as small as 3 grams or run up to 3 kilos or more.

Seven Sisters is an example of raw, loose-leaf pu-erh tea that has not been molded.

HERBAL "TEA"/TISANES

To be utterly correct, a beverage made from anything other than the leaves of *Camellia sinensis* should not be called a tea. We use the term "herbal tea" to cover a large group of beverages, even if they are not actually made from herbs (the leaves of aromatic edible plants) but bark, flowers, roots, or seeds. The French name for this type of brew is *tisane,* a word that appears on many restaurant beverage menus.

In addition to a huge range of enticing flavors, herbal tea is popular for two reasons. First, with the exception of yerba maté (described on page 20), herbal teas do not contain caffeine, and are perfect for those wishing to avoid this stimulant. Also, some tisanes have reputations for being especially effective digestive aids, so they are the ideal after-dinner beverage. When I was a student in Mexico, my tummyaches were not treated with medicine from a bottle, but with copious cups of *manzanilla* (chamomile) or *menta* (mint).

Herbal tea can be steeped according to taste to make a lightly or deeply flavored brew. Sweeten it with a bit of honey or sugar, if you like, but few of these infusions are good with milk. Here are some of the most popular tisanes:

CHAMOMILE, with its familiar applelike aroma, brews into a mild tea that is sometimes combined with stronger herbs, such as peppermint.

Clockwise from top left: **Chai, Hibiscus, Rooibos, Chrysanthemum.**

CHRYSANTHEMUM tea consists of the dried flowers, and is prized as a gift in Chinese culture.

HIBISCUS flowers (actually the sepals) are dried to brew into a delicious, if tart, magenta-colored tea. At Latino grocery stores, hibiscus may be labeled *flor de jamaica,* and Caribbean markets may sell it as sorrel or red sorrel. It is especially tasty when sweetened and iced.

OSMANTHUS, an evergreen shrub, has very aromatic blossoms that are used to add fragrance to black or green tea leaves in a manner similar to producing jasmine tea. The blossoms can also be tied with green or white tea leaves as a presentation tea.

PEPPERMINT makes an herbal tea that is equally good hot or iced. Fresh mint leaves are blended with green gunpowder tea to make the favorite tea of Morocco. The traditional Moroccan tea service is impressive, as the server pours the tea from a pot held at eye level into glasses a few feet below to create a foam.

ROOIBOS (pronounced ROY-bos), produced from a plant that only grows in South Africa, is called "red tea" by Westerners because both the leaves and brewed beverage are brownish-red. (What we call black tea, the Chinese call red tea.) The fresh rooibos leaves are black, but turn red after drying.

YERBA MATÉ, popular in Latin America, is unique among herbal teas because it contains caffeine. To minimize its natural bitter flavor, steep it in very hot, but not boiling, water until it is as strong as you like.

STORING TEA ❧

If stored correctly, green, oolong, and herbal teas will keep for about a year, and black tea for about two years. Pu-erh tea will keep indefinitely. At the opposite end of the tea spectrum, white tea should be served within a few months of purchase to best appreciate its fresh, delicate flavor.

Tea will grow stale more quickly when exposed to oxygen and light. To protect the tea from these factors, the best purveyors store their tea in metal containers. At home, store tea in an airtight container in a cool, dark place. Metal canisters are best because they are less permeable to oxygen than plastic. Do not freeze or refrigerate tea, as the tea can pick up the flavors of other foods or undesirable aromas.

BREWING TEA ❧

There is a tendency among tea lovers to dismiss tea bags as the worst thing that ever happened to tea. It is true that inexpensive tea bags are likely to contain the bits of broken leaves called "fannings" that are left over from processing whole leaves. And there is nothing romantic about wrapping your tea in cheap paper. Nonetheless, the convenience of tea bags cannot be disputed. Many top tea purveyors now offer their best teas in silk or nylon bags, a vast improvement over the old paper tea bags.

However, there is a single important reason that loose tea is preferable to tea bags. Tea leaves expand in hot water, and they need space to unfurl and come into contact with the water. Tea just doesn't like cramped quarters (the best tea bags provide plenty of "elbow room"). For ease of preparation, you can't beat tea bags, and they have their place. But whenever possible, make tea with loose leaves, and you are bound to notice a difference.

Without water, there would be no brewed tea. Tap water contains all sorts of additives (such as chlorine and mineral deposits) that can be tasted to varying degrees and will adversely affect brewed tea. For the best tea, use spring or filtered water. Note that not all bottled water is spring water, so read the label carefully. Don't use distilled water, as virtually all of the minerals have been removed, and some need to remain in the water to bring out the tea's flavor.

The water must be heated to brew the tea leaves. (Let's leave alternative methods, such as the "Not" Sun Tea on page 35, out of this discussion.) The temperature and steeping time vary for

each type of tea. Teas exposed to the incorrect water temperature or steeped too long can be bitter. Generally, less processed teas (white, green, and oolong) need lower water temperatures and shorter brewing times, and only black and herbal teas are brewed in water that is near boiling. Many tea producers now provide specific instructions for water temperature and steeping times with their tea. In the final analysis, brewing tea is a matter of personal taste, as some people prefer their tea stronger or lighter than others. Use the following chart for guidelines.

STEEPING SUGGESTIONS

Based on 6 to 8 ounces of water

TEA VARIETY	WHITE	GREEN	OOLONG	BLACK	PU-ERH	TISANE
WATER TEMPERATURE	180˚F	180˚F	190˚F	205˚F	205˚F	205˚F
STEEPING TIME	30 SEC TO 2 MINUTES	30 SEC TO 2 MINUTES	3 TO 4 MINUTES	3 TO 4 MINUTES	3 TO 5 MINUTES	4 TO 5 MINUTES
AMOUNT OF TEA	1 TO 1½ TEASPOONS	1 TO 1½ TEASPOONS	1 TEASPOON	1 TEASPOON	1 TO 1½ TEASPOONS	2 TEASPOONS

Courtesy of Admari Tea, www.admaritea.com

Also, some teas (in particular, white, green, and some oolong varieties) are meant to be enjoyed in several consecutive brewings. The tea is brewed in a very small pot and poured into cups that hold just a couple of sips. Each brewing will have a subtle flavor change, with the third and fourth brewings usually the strongest. Again, your purveyor will guide you in the specifics for each tea. These are definitely teas for contemplation and sharing with other tea aficionados in a kind of streamlined tea ceremony.

Start your tea brewing by filling the teapot with very hot tap water, and let stand for a few minutes to warm it. If you wish, you can warm the cups as well. In the meantime, pour water into a kettle or saucepan, allowing ¾ to 1 cup water per serving, depending on how strong you like your tea, and heat over high. Many tea lovers find that microwaved water makes a flat-tasting tea, so stick to the time-honored method of water boiled on the stove.

Whether or not the water should come to a full boil before adding it to the tea is a matter of dispute among tea lovers. Some contend that the Chinese are right in letting the water come to a full boil to "open the water." Others say that you should merely heat the water to the desired temperature, even if it doesn't reach a boil. If you go the "full boil" method, remove the water from the heat as soon as it reaches that point, as long boiling depletes the oxygen in the water, and your tea will taste flat instead of vibrant. The important point to remember is that tea can be damaged by using water that is too hot for the specific variety.

Personally, I always bring the water to a full boil, and then go from there. For delicate green, white, and oolong teas, bring the water to a boil in a saucepan, rather than a teakettle, to help it cool more quickly after boiling before adding to the leaves. A wait of about a minute, stirring the water occasionally to speed cooling, is sufficient. When brewing black, pu-erh, and tisanes, use a teakettle to bring water just to a full rolling boil. Even then, cool the water slightly for about 15 seconds before using, and avoid pouring sputtering water over the leaves. A thermometer is unnecessary—approximate temperatures are fine.

Empty the water from the pot, and add the tea leaves to the pot. The common practice is to use 1 rounded teaspoon (a teaspoon from a place setting, not a measuring spoon) per serving. For more than 4 servings, add 1 additional teaspoon "for the pot." If you wish, put the leaves in a tea ball, which will contain the leaves and keep them from clogging the spout during pouring, but don't overpack so the leaves have room for expansion. Pour in the hot water (cooled as needed), cover the pot, and let steep for the desired period.

Now is the time to discard the water from the warmed cups. Pour the tea into the cups, using a tea strainer to hold back the leaves, if needed. Add sweetener, milk, or lemon as you wish. If you are serving tea to guests at a special occasion, a little foresight will upgrade the experience. Use demerara sugar (a lightly refined sugar with golden, roughly shaped crystals and a lovely caramel flavor), sugar cubes, or honey instead of plain sugar for a more elegant presentation. Milk is preferable to half-and-half, as cream masks the flavor of the tea. Tie the lemon wedges in small pieces of cheesecloth to hold back the seeds.

HOT AND COLD TEA BEVERAGES

A cup of hot tea can soothe as well as revive, and iced tea is a well-known refresher. You probably have your favorite way to enjoy tea, but here are some new ways to make the beverage, featuring the beloved flavors of ginger, pomegranate, cinnamon, and even chocolate.

❧ ORANGE SPICE TEA

There are plenty of orange-and-spice-flavored teas on the market,
but it is such a pleasure to personalize your cup. Enjoy it sip by aromatic sip.

1 orange

One 3-inch cinnamon stick,
broken in half lengthwise

1 star anise

6 whole cloves

2 rounded teaspoons black tea leaves,
such as English Breakfast

1. Using a vegetable peeler, remove two 3-inch strips of zest from the orange. Juice the orange and measure out ¼ cup of the juice.

2. In a small saucepan, combine 1½ cups water with the orange juice and zest, cinnamon, star anise, and cloves. Let the mixture come to a boil slowly over medium-low heat so the spices can infuse the water. Meanwhile, fill a small teapot with hot tap water and let stand to heat the pot.

3. Discard the water in the teapot. Add the tea to the teapot. Pour in the contents of the saucepan, including the spices and zest. Cover and steep for 3 to 4 minutes. Pour through a tea strainer into two cups and serve hot.

POMEGRANATE MINT TEA

Here's another suggestion for a flavored tea, this time using a combination of ingredients beloved in Middle Eastern cuisine. Pomegranate juice is enjoying newfound popularity for its tart flavor and antioxidant properties, and I usually have a bottle in the refrigerator. Add some mint from the garden, and the result is this wonderful hot beverage.

Six 3-inch mint sprigs

½ cup bottled pomegranate juice

2 rounded teaspoons oolong tea leaves

1. Crush the mint between your fingers and put it in a small saucepan. Add 1 cup water and the pomegranate juice. Let the mixture come to a boil slowly over medium-low heat so the mint can infuse the water. Meanwhile, fill a small teapot with hot tap water and let stand to heat the pot.

2. Discard the water in the teapot. Add the tea to the teapot. Pour in the contents of the saucepan, including the mint. Cover and steep for 3 to 4 minutes. Pour through a tea strainer into two cups and serve hot.

GINGERED GREEN TEA

This tea is lovely by itself, but it is also excellent as a beverage with savory Asian food. Gunpowder green tea, which has an assertiveness of its own, is a good match for the ginger flavor. Although I usually pass on sweetening my tea, a bit of honey can be welcome here.

Six ¼-inch-thick slices fresh ginger
(no need to peel the ginger)

2 heaping teaspoons
Chinese green tea leaves,
such as gunpowder

1. Crush 4 ginger slices under a knife. Combine 1½ cups water and the ginger in a small saucepan. Let the water come to a boil slowly over medium-low heat so the ginger can infuse the water. Meanwhile, fill a small teapot with hot tap water and let stand to heat the pot.

2. Discard the water in the teapot. Add the tea to the teapot. Remove the ginger from the water and discard. Pour the boiling water into the teapot. Cover and steep for about 3 minutes. Pour through a tea strainer into two cups. Add a whole, uncrushed ginger slice to each serving and serve hot.

❧ CLASSIC CHAI

In Hindi, *chai* is the generic word for tea. Spiced tea is *masala chai*, although Westerners incorrectly shorten it to chai. While my version of chai has the expected Indian flavors, there is really no single way to prepare this milky drink. You may want to make a double batch, as it will keep in the refrigerator for a couple of days and can be reheated or served over ice.

One 3-inch cinnamon stick

8 black peppercorns

3 cardamom pods, crushed

4 whole cloves

1 cup whole milk

2 rounded teaspoons Indian black tea, such as Assam

Sugar (optional)

1. Combine 1 cup water with the cinnamon, peppercorns, cardamom, and cloves in a small saucepan. Let the water come to a boil slowly over medium-low heat so the spices can infuse the water.

2. Add the milk and the tea. Heat, stirring constantly, until piping hot but not boiling, about 3 minutes. Strain into mugs and serve hot with sugar, if desired.

"NOT" SUN TEA ❧

Combine tea and water, stick it in the sun, and let it steep. That's all there is to sun tea, right? Actually, soaking tea leaves in unboiled water in the sun is the perfect recipe for growing bacteria. Steeping tea in the refrigerator is a much safer plan—sunlight is not a magic ingredient to brew tea in cold water. When the tea is ready to serve, transfer it to your favorite iced tea container to get an old-fashioned look with new-fashioned sensibility.

¼ cup black tea leaves, such as English Breakfast

Fresh mint or lemon verbena sprigs (optional)

Frozen tea cubes (see page 39) for serving

Simple Syrup (page 36) for serving

1. Combine 1 quart cold water and the tea leaves in a pitcher. Add the mint or lemon verbena sprigs to taste, if using. Cover and refrigerate for at least 4 hours or overnight.

2. Serve, poured over the frozen tea cubes, with the syrup passed on the side.

SIMPLE SYRUP

MAKES ABOUT 1¼ CUPS

Stirring granulated sugar into a tall glass of iced tea is an exercise in frustration—the sugar just won't dissolve. Bartenders' (also called superfine) sugar, which dissolves instantly in iced beverages, works, but there is a much more elegant way. It's called simple syrup.

Simple syrup is just sugar boiled with water to make a liquid perfect for sweetening up iced beverages. It will keep in the refrigerator for a few weeks. At my house during the summer, the syrup is stored in a tall bottle with a pouring spout, and it finds its way into the obvious iced tea and coffee. It also makes a great quick lemonade, mixed with fresh lemon juice and water.

For flavored syrup, add ⅓ cup packed fresh mint or lemon verbena leaves to the syrup when it comes off the stove. When cooled, strain out the leaves.

1 cup granulated sugar

1. Combine the sugar and 1 cup water in a small saucepan. Bring to a boil over high heat, stirring often to dissolve the sugar. Reduce the heat to low and simmer for 1 minute. Remove from the heat and let cool completely.

2. Transfer to a covered container or a bottle with a pouring spout and refrigerate. (The syrup can be stored in the refrigerator for up to 1 month.)

ROOIBOS HOT COCOA 🌿

Rooibos has a warm flavor that reminds some drinkers of cinnamon, making it the perfect choice for blending with hot cocoa. If you have a rooibos tea bag, use it instead of the loose leaf to skip the straining—just remove the bag from the milk after steeping.

1½ teaspoons unsweetened cocoa powder

2 teaspoons sugar

1 cup whole milk

1 heaping teaspoon rooibos

⅛ teaspoon vanilla extract

1. Bring about ¼ cup water to a boil in a small saucepan over high heat. Combine the cocoa and sugar in a mug. Add enough of the boiling water (about 1 tablespoon) to make a thin paste. Discard the remaining water.

2. Combine the milk and rooibos in the saucepan, and bring to a simmer over high heat. Remove from the heat, cover, and let steep for 5 minutes. Add the vanilla. Strain through a fine-mesh wire sieve into a liquid measuring cup (the same one you used for the milk).

3. Pour the hot milk mixture into the mug and stir well. Serve hot.

✺ MANGO TEA SLUSH

With frozen tea cubes in the freezer, you can make this incredibly refreshing drink in a few minutes. Mango brings its exotic fragrance and tropical flavor to the proceedings. Try it with other fruits, such as raspberries or peaches.

1 ripe mango

1 cup (8 cubes, about 2 tablespoons each) frozen black tea cubes (see opposite page)

⅓ cup orange juice, preferably fresh

2 tablespoons honey

1. Place the mango on a work surface. The pit, which is about ½ inch thick, will run horizontally through the center of the fruit. Use a sharp knife to cut off the top of the fruit, coming just above the top of the pit. Turn the mango over and cut off the other side of the fruit. Using a large metal serving spoon, scoop the mango flesh out of each portion in one piece. The pit portion can be pared with a small knife, and the flesh nibbled from the pit as the cook's treat.

2. Combine the mango, frozen tea cubes, orange juice, and honey in a blender. Process, stopping the machine and stirring the mixture as needed, until smooth and slushy. Pour into two tall glasses and serve immediately.

FROZEN TEA CUBES

One of the great pleasures of summertime, iced tea can be as refreshing as a dip in a cool stream. But like anything that stands in the hot summer sun, iced tea can quickly become heated. Load up the glass with more ice cubes, and the tea just becomes diluted beyond recognition.

Instead of using cubes of frozen water, use frozen tea cubes. They will chill your tea just as well as the water cubes, but when they melt, the drink won't get watered down.

Make the tea cubes from the same tea that you usually use for iced tea. Just brew a batch, let it cool, and pour into ice cube trays. After the cubes are frozen, pop them out of the trays and store in zippered plastic storage bags.

For a fancy summertime tea party, make decorative tea cubes. Fill each cube halfway with tea (or water) and freeze until solid. Place a blueberry or raspberry in each cube mold, fill with more tea, and freeze until the top layer is solid. You can also make floral ice cubes with edible blossoms, substituting johnny-jump-ups or marigold petals for the berries.

Beyond their main job of icing cold drinks, plain iced tea cubes can also be tossed in the blender with fruit or juices to make cooling slushes. As there is no standard size for capacity of ice cube molds, you may have to adjust the amount of cubes needed to get the consistency you want. (Each mold in my ice cube tray holds about 2 tablespoons.)

❧ PEACHY ICED TEA COOLER

When peaches are in season, I look to use them in as many ways as possible. This drink was created as a nonalcoholic version of the Bellini, the beloved peach-and-Prosecco cocktail that hails from Venice. For the best results, use a high-quality ginger ale or imported ginger beer, as these have a stronger flavor than the typical supermarket soda.

1 ripe white or yellow peach

1 teaspoon fresh lemon juice

1 teaspoon superfine or granulated sugar

Frozen tea cubes (see page 39) for serving

1 cup "Not" Sun Tea (page 35)

One 12-ounce bottle chilled ginger ale or ginger beer

1. Using a vegetable peeler, peel the peach. (Use a moderate amount of pressure, and go around the circumference of the peach with a slight sawing up-and-down motion. This is quicker than the usual method of blanching the peach in boiling water.) Cut the peach in half and remove the pit. Coarsely chop the peach flesh. Transfer to a blender, add the lemon juice and sugar, and puree. Transfer to a covered container and refrigerate until ready to use. (The puree can be made up to 2 hours ahead.)

2. Pour the peach puree into two tall glasses. Fill with the frozen tea cubes. Pour equal amounts of the iced tea into each glass. Top each with about ¼ cup of the ginger ale (save the remaining ginger ale for another use) and serve chilled.

HIBISCUS AGUA FRESCA

I first learned to love *agua fresca de flor de jamaica,* the Mexican answer to iced tea, during my sojourn at the University of Guadalajara. It is quite tart on its own and is always sweetened, but you could make it unsweetened and serve simple syrup on the side so each guest can add the syrup to taste.

½ cup dried hibiscus flowers (*flor de jamaica*)

½ cup sugar

Ice cubes for serving

Lime wedges for serving

Simple Syrup (page 36) for serving

1. Bring 2 quarts water to a boil in a large saucepan over high heat. Remove from the heat, add the hibiscus flowers and sugar, and stir to dissolve the sugar. Let stand 10 minutes.

2. Strain into a heatproof pitcher and cool to room temperature. Serve over ice, garnished with lime wedges, with the syrup on the side.

CARIBBEAN SORREL PUNCH in Jamaica and other parts of the Caribbean, the hibiscus "tea" is flavored with ginger. Add 8 quarter-size slices of fresh ginger, crushed under a knife, to the water before boiling.

❦ HALF-AND-HALF

Whoever thought up the combination of lemonade and iced tea is to be commended (its invention is attributed to Arnold Palmer). There are few more thirst-quenching drinks under the sun, and this one is especially useful at summer parties as an alternative to alcoholic beverages. Rather than make separate batches of lemonade and tea, here's how I prepare it in one fell swoop. To simplify the chore of juicing the lemons, buy an inexpensive electric citrus juicer.

⅓ cup plus 1 tablespoon sugar

4 rounded teaspoons black tea leaves, such as English Breakfast

½ cup fresh lemon juice (about 3 lemons)

Frozen tea cubes (see page 39) for serving

Fresh mint sprigs for garnish

1. In a medium saucepan over high heat, bring 4 cups water and the sugar to a boil, stirring to dissolve the sugar.

2. Add the tea and let steep for 4 to 5 minutes. (This goes against the usual advice to always add water to tea and not the other way around, but it doesn't make enough of a flavor difference here to bother with methods that would require extra utensils.) Stir in the lemon juice.

3. Strain into a heatproof pitcher. Let cool. Serve over frozen tea cubes, garnishing each glass with a mint sprig.

FRUITY BUBBLE TEA

Bubble tea, also called boba or pearl tea (among many other names), is a lot of fun to make. You will need to make a trip to an Asian grocery store to find the tapioca pearls (regular pearl tapioca doesn't work) and wide straws used to slurp up the "bubbles," or shop online at www.bobateadirect.com. As adding ice cubes will cause some dilution, make this tea on the strong side. Change the drink by varying the fruit-flavored tea and matching syrup.

3 tablespoons pearl tapioca for bubble tea

Simple Syrup (page 36), as needed

3 rounded teaspoons fruit-flavored black tea, such as mango or passion fruit

2 tablespoons fruit-flavored beverage syrup, such as mango or passion fruit

½ cup whole milk

Ice cubes

1. To prepare the tapioca "bubbles," bring 1½ cups water to a boil over high heat in a small saucepan. Add the tapioca and reduce the heat to medium-low. Simmer until the tapioca is barely tender, about 30 minutes. Remove from the heat, cover, and let stand for 30 minutes. Drain in a wire sieve and rinse under cold water. Transfer to a small bowl and add enough simple syrup to cover. Let cool, but use within 6 hours.

2. Bring 2 cups water to a boil over high heat. Add the tea to a teapot and add the hot water. Let stand 5 minutes. Pour the tea through a tea strainer into a heatproof pitcher. Let cool.

3. Fill a cocktail shaker with ice cubes. Add the cooled tea, beverage syrup, and milk. Place the lid on the shaker and cover. Shake well until the mixture is foamy. Add more simple or beverage syrup to taste. Divide the tapioca bubbles between two tall glasses. Pour the tea and ice cubes into the glasses. Serve chilled, with wide straws for slurping up the tapioca bubbles.

A COOKIE
PRIMER

When I was a beginning baker, my cookies were generally acceptable, but I was often confused by their behavior. Sometimes they were perfect. Other times, they spread out like pancakes on the baking sheet, or they were too toasty on the bottoms. Because they were still edible, I didn't analyze the situation. For nostalgia's sake, I clung to the way my family taught me to bake cookies. I refused to chuck my grandmother's thin cookie sheets for sturdy half-sheet pans, and to ditch the chore of greasing and flouring the sheets for the ease of lining them with parchment paper. I still creamed butter and sugar with a wooden spoon, because that was the way Grandma did it.

When I received a call to help a cookbook-author friend test cookie recipes for her cookbook, she convinced me that my cookie skills needed an attitude adjustment. Armed with new half-sheet baking pans and a stack of parchment paper, I discovered how the right equipment can make the difference between good cookies and great ones. And, faced with the challenge of baking scores of cookie recipes, one after the other, I was forced to observe the fine points of the genre. What follows is a primer of what I have learned about these sweet little morsels over the years.

INGREDIENTS

Cookies could be thought of as small cakes. Of course, the main difference is, cakes are molded in pans, but most cookies are not. Nonetheless, cookies and cakes share many of the same ingredients. Here is a glossary of common baking ingredients, and suggestions for their use when making cookies.

FLOUR

Flour is the backbone of all cookie recipes. Milled from wheat, flour is mostly starch, but also contains proteins. These proteins give structure to baked goods—without them, the cake would collapse. When two of these proteins, gliadin and glutenin, are moistened with water and mixed, they form gluten, an invisible system in the dough. Manipulating the dough strengthens the gluten structure.

Bread dough is kneaded to create a strong gluten structure for chewy, crusty bread. When it comes to cookies, the batter should be mixed just long enough to incorporate the flour, keeping gluten formation at a minimum to avoid tough cookies. (In some cases, such as madeleines, the flour is only folded in, and not mixed at all.)

Professionals designate flour as "hard" or "soft," depending on the amount of potential gluten in the flour. Bread bakers prefer hard flour because their dough must have a strong gluten structure that can withstand kneading, and bake into bread with a crisp crust and chewy texture. Bread flour and unbleached flour are considered hard flours. Cake and pastry flours, with a low gluten content, are considered soft flours.

ALL-PURPOSE FLOUR is a combination of hard and soft flours. UNBLEACHED ALL-PURPOSE FLOUR has had the hull and bran removed before milling, and it has a relatively high protein content. BLEACHED ALL-PURPOSE FLOUR has been chemically treated to lengthen its shelf life, a process that also reduces the protein. Bleached flour makes for slightly more tender baked goods, but you can use unbleached if you prefer.

The flour in this book was measured by the dip-and-sweep method (see page 56).

BUTTER

There is no substitute for the creamy flavor of butter, and it is also an important building block in cookie dough. Mixing aerates the butter to create air bubbles that are part of the leavening process.

Butter is available unsalted or salted. Unsalted butter is best because the baker is in control over how much salt will be added to the recipe. Salt was originally added to butter to cover up any off flavors and to improve its shelf life, neither of which is an especially positive improvement.

When the butter will be creamed, the recipe's ingredient list instructs to have the butter "at room temperature." This is a useful phrase, but not entirely accurate, unless your kitchen is exactly 68°F, which is the optimum temperature for beating air into the butter during the creaming process. The butter should stand at room temperature until it has a malleable, almost plastic consistency, with a dull, not shiny, appearance. In general, this takes about 30 minutes for a stick of butter. One of the most common baking mistakes occurs when the butter is too soft, reducing the number of bubbles that can be created and resulting in an under-risen cake.

If you don't have the time to let the cold butter stand at room temperature and soften on its own, there are options. Cut the butter into ½-inch cubes and put them in a warm spot near the oven for about 15 minutes (meanwhile you can preheat the oven, assemble the ingredients, and prepare the pan). Or grate the chilled butter on the large holes of a box grater into the mixing bowl. Do not use a microwave, as it is too easy to melt and not soften the butter.

EGGS

Eggs moisten the batter and give it an elasticity that traps air and contributes to rising. The eggs should be at room temperature, which makes them more easily absorbed into the batter. The discrepancy in temperature between the creamed mixture and chilled eggs can cause curdling. And room-temperature eggs have the best elasticity and ability to expand when beaten.

To quickly bring cold eggs to room temperature, place the uncracked eggs in a bowl, cover with hot tap water, and let stand for about 5 minutes. Eggs are easier to separate when they are chilled. For separated eggs, place the yolks and whites in separate bowls, place each bowl in a larger bowl of warm water, and let stand until the contents lose their chill, about 5 minutes.

DRIED EGG WHITES are used to make royal icing, the slick and shiny coating that decorates sugar cookies. This icing was originally made with raw egg whites, which many bakers prefer to avoid because of the possibility of salmonella contamination. You'll find dried egg whites at well-stocked supermarkets. MERINGUE POWDER, which is dried egg whites with sugar and stabilizers added, is available at cake decorating suppliers and hobby shops and can be substituted for the dried egg whites. Both of these products need to be reconstituted with water. You can also make royal icing with liquid egg whites, sold in cartons from the refrigerated section of the market. Like the dried products, LIQUID EGG WHITES are pasteurized and safe to use for the uncooked icing.

SUGAR

Classic cookies use sugar as the main sweetener. Sugar can be processed from either sugar cane or sugar beets, but most bakers have a strong preference for cane sugar, as beet sugar doesn't behave reliably in all applications (such as melting to make caramel). Look for the words "cane sugar" on the packaging. GRANULATED SUGAR, with medium-size crystals, is the sugar most often used for cookie dough.

CONFECTIONERS' SUGAR, also called powdered sugar, is finely ground sugar with a little cornstarch added to discourage clumping. Used for icings and frostings and for decorating, it is usually sifted first to remove lumps.

BROWN SUGAR used to be a by-product of the sugar-making process, but these days it is usually just crystallized sugar that has been sprayed with molasses for flavor and color. The amount of molasses creates light or dark sugar, which are interchangeable, depending on how much molasses flavor you like. MUSCOVADO SUGAR is brown sugar made by the traditional methods, a factor that adds to its cost. Always store brown sugar in an airtight container to keep it from absorbing moisture from the air and clumping. Don't use lumpy brown sugar in cookie dough, as the baked cookies will be dotted with undissolved brown sugar. To return lumpy brown sugar to its original state, rub it through a coarse-mesh wire sieve to break down the lumps.

LEAVENING

The two most common leavenings for cookies are baking powder and baking soda. (A third leavening, yeast, is not used in this book.) During mixing, tiny air bubbles are incorporated into the cookie dough. The leavenings create carbon dioxide to inflate the bubbles, making the dough rise.

BAKING SODA (bicarbonate of soda) is an alkali. Mix it with an acidic ingredient (such as buttermilk, sour cream, vinegar, lemon juice, brown sugar, molasses, or natural cocoa powder), moisten it, and carbon dioxide forms.

BAKING POWDER does not need an acidic ingredient to be activated. It is made of baking soda combined with a dry acidic ingredient (usually aluminum sodium sulfate). When moistened, the baking powder creates carbon dioxide to make the cookies rise. Commercial baking powder is almost always labeled "double-acting," which means that the baking powder is initially activated when moistened, but the heat of the oven creates a second burst of leavening the batter. Some bakers, including me, find that since baking powders with aluminum by-products have a bitter flavor that can be detected in baked goods, it is better to buy aluminum-free baking powder. Rumford's is my preferred brand.

There are recipes that use both baking soda and baking powder. The soda acts to neutralize the acid ingredients, providing a small amount of the leavening in the process, while the baking powder does the bulk of the work.

MILK

All ingredients for cookie dough should be at room temperature for the most efficient mixing. Milk is no exception. Let the measured milk stand at room temperature for about an hour so it loses its chill, or place the measuring cup in a bowl of hot water for a few minutes. Or microwave it in a microwave-safe container on low (20 percent power) in 10-second periods, stirring after each increment, until the milk is tepid.

WHOLE MILK, which contains fat, is the best choice for cookie dough. The cookies could be tough if reduced, low-, or nonfat milk is used instead.

SALT

Without a little salt in the batter, cookies can taste flat. This is especially true of chocolate cookies. In cookie dough, salt is used sparingly as a flavor enhancer and is not a prominent taste itself, so the most important factor is how easily the salt dissolves. (This isn't the case in savory cooking, where coarse salt can be purposely used to add texture to a dish.) Fine sea salt, which has a clean, neutral flavor, is my first choice, but plain table salt will also work well. Kosher salt is too coarse and its large crystals don't dissolve well. If you only have coarse salt in your kitchen, grind it first in a spice grinder or mortar and pestle before using in baking.

CHOCOLATE AND COCOA

One of the world's most beloved foods, for all its ubiquity, chocolate is a fairly complex subject. UNSWEETENED CHOCOLATE is cacao beans that have been roasted, ground, molded, and cooled. Professionals sometimes call it "chocolate liquor." It contains no sugar.

SEMISWEET OR BITTERSWEET CHOCOLATE is chocolate liquor that has been sweetened to some degree. The USDA doesn't have a specific standard for semisweet or bittersweet chocolate, and only has a category for dark chocolate, meaning any chocolate with a minimum of 35 percent cacao. This is fairly meaningless, because no producers make chocolate with such low cacao content. The average cacao content in semisweet chocolate is around 55 percent, with the remaining contents being sugar, the emulsifier lecithin, and vanilla (or the artificial alternative, vanillin). However, one brand's semisweet can be another's bittersweet. Many chocolate brands now state the cacao percentage on the label. If it isn't listed, you can assume that it isn't above 62 percent. I use Callebaut semisweet chocolate, which is easily found in bulk at many natural food stores and supermarkets, for my "house chocolate." Trader Joe's also carries excellent, reasonably priced Belgian bulk chocolate.

HIGH-PERCENTAGE CHOCOLATE has a larger proportion of cacao, which naturally gives it a deeper chocolate flavor. If you like a bitter note to your eating chocolate, you will like high-percentage chocolate. But it can make trouble in baking. The cacao content can wreak havoc with a recipe, as the proportions of sugar and other ingredients (such as the fat supplied by cocoa butter in the chocolate) are thrown off. This is especially true of ganache, a combination of heavy cream and chocolate, which depends on a precise balance of butterfat and cocoa butter for its success. For this reason, I recommend chocolate with a cacao content of no higher than 62 percent.

MILK CHOCOLATE is sweeter than semisweet chocolate and has been flavored with dried milk solids. WHITE CHOCOLATE contains no cacao at all; in fact the best brands are basically sweetened cocoa butter flavored with vanilla. Both of these chocolates are delicate and can scorch easily, so melt them with an extra measure of caution.

CHOCOLATE CHIPS are processed with an additional amount of lecithin to keep them from melting too quickly in the oven.

Before using, chop chocolate into small pieces with a serrated knife. The serrated knife grips the chocolate better than a straight-edged one, and you have less chance of cutting yourself. Do not chop chocolate in a food processor, as the friction can heat and melt the chocolate. And while it may be tempting to use chocolate chips to skip the chore of chopping the chocolate, the extra lecithin in the chips makes them difficult to melt. If you bake a lot and want to save time from chopping, look for chocolate *callets* or *pistoles,* small disks of chocolate made expressly for melting.

In these recipes, chocolate is always combined with a warm ingredient (usually melted butter or cream) to melt it. This is less complicated than melting chocolate by itself, but it doesn't mean that the baker can be careless. When chocolate is overheated, it thickens and becomes lumpy. Each recipe provides instructions to avoid overheating.

COCOA POWDER is pulverized, unsweetened cacao beans. NATURAL COCOA POWDER, such as the familiar Hershey's in the brown box, is the cocoa that Americans always baked with in the past because nothing else was readily available. It is acidic, and recipes that use it usually call for baking soda to neutralize it. DUTCH-PROCESSED COCOA has been treated with alkali to reduce its acidity and deepen its color (the procedure was invented in the Netherlands in the 1830s). If a recipe calls for Dutch-processed cocoa, it can be leavened with baking powder, as the acidity of the cocoa has been reduced so much that baking soda isn't needed to neutralize it.

Always use the cocoa called for in the recipe. When I am developing recipes with cocoa, I usually opt for natural cocoa for a traditional American flavor and Dutch-processed cocoa for darker color. I have used natural cocoa powder in most of the recipes in this book. In the cases where there is a choice between the two cocoas, I have recommended Dutch-processed cocoa for its coloring properties, but natural cocoa will work as well.

VANILLA

If you have ever wondered why vanilla is relatively expensive, consider this: The vanilla orchid, which only grows in tropical regions, must be hand-pollinated for commercial use, and the flower only opens one day a year. The good news for bakers is that vanilla is used in small amounts, so your investment lasts a long time.

Vanilla beans and their seeds are often used to flavor custards, ice creams, sweet fillings, and desserts or their components, but the beans' delicate aroma and flavor can be lost in cookie dough unless the baker uses an inordinate amount. Vanilla extract is the more effective and common way to infuse vanilla flavor into baked goods. Imitation vanilla extract (vanillin) is a by-product of paper manufacturing, reason enough not to use it. However, more than one taste panel has determined that there is little flavor difference between real and artificial vanilla. So, while I prefer to stick with the real thing, the choice is yours.

High-quality vanilla extract often has its beans' source on the label. Madagascar-Bourbon indicates that the beans come from two of the most highly regarded locations for vanilla plantations (Bourbon is the former name of the island of Réunion). Mexican vanilla is very similar in flavor. Tahitian vanilla has a distinctive, perfumed aroma. Again, although I like the full rounded flavor of Madagascar-Bourbon, there is room for personal preferences.

FOOD COLORING

A judicious drop of food coloring can give food an appetizing tint. The adage "we eat with our eyes" is true, and adjusting the color of *macarons* from beige to pale yellow makes them more attractive and sends a signal that the cookies will be lemon flavored. This is also the reason I've tinted my pistachio meringue cookies pastel green.

Food coloring comes in three forms: gel, paste, and liquid. Gel, which gives deep, rich colors, is my favorite. It gives much brighter colors than liquid and is more convenient to use than paste, which must be removed from the jar in minuscule amounts with the tip of a toothpick. Just squeeze the gel from its bottle, a drop at a time, into the food and stir to distribute well. Gauge the color carefully, as the gel is so concentrated that it is easy to go overboard and make the tint *too* saturated. My preferred brand is Spectrum, made by Ateco, as its colors are very attractive. You can find individual hues or a six- or twelve-pack of the most popular colors in small plastic bottles at cake decorating suppliers and hobby shops. Food colorings with all-natural ingredients are available at natural food grocery stores, but you may find the colors to be muted.

MEASURING

☙

Bakers love to argue about measuring, especially when it comes to flour, as its fluffy texture makes it susceptible to variations in measurement methods. Professional bakers always weigh their dry ingredients, while most home bakers prefer measuring cups. After interviewing many of my baking students in my classes around the country, I know that the vast majority of home bakers don't own an electric scale, and that they are going to use volume measurements anyway. Therefore, I provide volume measurements only here.

That being said, there is another problem with volume measuring that must be addressed. Some bakers spoon the flour into a measuring cup, and others simply dip the cup into the flour's container to fill the cup. Each method gives a different weight. The flour in this book has been measured by the "dip-and-sweep" method. Dip a dry-ingredient (metal or plastic) cup into the flour to fill it. Take care that there are no air pockets in the cup, but don't pack the flour. Sweep away the excess flour with the edge of a knife so the flour remaining in the cup is level with the cup's edge.

EQUIPMENT

OVENS

Take it from me—ovens are notoriously unreliable. In the last five years, I have had three brand-name ovens in my kitchen, and only one heated to a temperature within an acceptable range of the number set on the thermostat.

For accuracy's sake, always test the oven temperature with an **OVEN THERMOMETER**. The best thermometers have alcohol-filled glass gauges, but dial-type thermometers can be good, too. The most important factor is the visibility of the numbers. Place the thermometer in the center of the oven rack, well away from the sides.

Many ovens have the option for convection baking, but most of the home cooks I know are simply afraid of it. Convection baking uses a fan to circulate the hot air in the oven, which promotes browning and cooks food more quickly. When using convection baking, decrease the standard temperature in a recipe by 25°F, and estimate that the cookies will bake in about two-thirds of the conventional baking time. You will have to rely on visual and touch tests to check for doneness, but that's a good idea for any kind of cooking, whether or not convection is used.

ELECTRIC MIXERS

A **HEAVY-DUTY STANDING ELECTRIC MIXER** has become standard in the passionate home baker's kitchen. Cookie bakers will use the paddle-blade attachment for creaming butter and sugar and subsequent dough mixing, and the whisk attachment for preparing royal icing for decorating. (The dough hook is reserved for kneading bread dough in the work bowl.) The 5-quart model is the most versatile size, and its motor is strong enough to mix cookie dough from start to finish. When adding the flour at the end, be sure to turn the mixer speed to low, or simply stir it in with a wooden spoon.

If you don't have a standing mixer, all the recipes in this book can be made with an **ELECTRIC HAND MIXER**. The only caveat is that a hand mixer may not be strong enough for mixing in the flour. In that case, stop the mixer and stir in the flour by hand with a sturdy wooden spoon. And in cases where there aren't enough ingredients to sufficiently fill a standing mixer, the hand mixer is a must.

BAKING SHEETS AND PANS

The majority of cookies in this book are baked on baking sheets. **HALF-SHEET PANS**, which measure about 18 x 13 inches and are made from sturdy aluminum, are the choice of professional bakers, and I used them to test these recipes. (I have no idea why they are called pans when they are only 1 inch deep. A full-sheet pan, used in professional kitchens, measures 26 x 18 inches, so now you know where the term "half-sheet" originated.)

As I stated in the introduction, I made excuses for not buying half-sheet pans, but as soon as I made the change, most of my serious cookie-baking problems disappeared. Half-sheet pans are easy to find at kitchenware shops, but you'll find the best prices at restaurant suppliers. Buy as many sheets as you have room for in your kitchen (at least two), as you can never have too many baking sheets when holiday baking time rolls around. And they come in handy for savory cooking too, such as roasting vegetables.

Traditional cookie sheets are too thin and they darken with use, and as dark colors absorb oven heat more readily than shiny surfaces, cookies baked on them cook more quickly and can scorch. Also, cookie sheets don't hold as many cookies as half-sheet pans, lengthening the time needed to complete a batch. Furthermore the cheap sheets tend to warp. You may find double-thick insulated cookie sheets, but these actually discourage crisp bottoms, so they aren't right for every cookie.

For bar cookies, I use 9 x 13-inch oblong and 8-inch square pans. I prefer metal pans as they reflect oven heat and bake evenly. Pyrex pans absorb oven heat, so if you use them, reduce the oven temperature by 25°F and keep a close eye on the cookies to avoid overbrowning. For some shallow bar cookies, I also use a QUARTER-SHEET PAN, measuring about 13 x 9 inches, a size that I have found to be as useful as its big sibling, the half-sheet.

For special cookies that require molding, I bake shortbread cookies in a 9-inch springform pan and madeleines in their specific pan with scallop-shell indentations. You will need two mini-muffin pans (measuring 1⅞ inches across the top and ⅞ inch deep) for the Candied Walnut Tassies (page 121).

UTENSILS AND TOOLS

A COARSE-MESH WIRE SIEVE does a great job of sifting dry ingredients. Do not use a fine-mesh sieve, which should be reserved for straining the tiny seeds from raspberry puree and the like.

Rubber (or silicone) spatulas are used to scrape ingredients down from the sides of a bowl during mixing, or to transfer every bit of batter from the bowl to the cake pan. Silicone spatulas are heat-resistant (some up to 800°F), so they are perfect for cooking and stirring hot ingredients on the stove, especially sticky ones that need to be occasionally scraped from the sides of the saucepan.

Many cookie recipes call for shaping the dough into 1-inch balls. To portion the dough quickly, use a small, stainless-steel spring-loaded ice-cream scoop with a .5 ounce (1 tablespoon) capacity. These are available at restaurant suppliers, many kitchenware stores, and online at www.surlatable.com. You may also see plastic scoops designed just for portioning cookie dough, and they work fine as well.

You'll use a rolling pin for rolling out dough for cut-out cookies such as Alfajores (page 106) and Sugar Cookie Teapots (page 123). The heavier the pin, the better, as the weight does much of the work for you. I love my silicone ball-bearing rolling pin because its surface doesn't stick to sugary doughs.

A large offset metal spatula is the tool for evenly spreading soft dough for brownies or blondies in the pan. Use a small offset spatula when icing sugar cookies.

Wire cake racks give the baker someplace to cool the cookies. The truth is that most cookies can be cooled directly on their baking sheets—they will not overbake. However, many bakers don't own more than two baking sheets and must remove the cookies from the sheets in order to bake more, so cooling racks are not entirely optional. Large rectangular racks can easily hold a large batch of cookies. For holiday baking when you may be making lots of cookies, or if you have a small kitchen with limited counter space, stackable cooling racks are great space savers.

Bakers love parchment paper for its nonstick and heat-resistant properties. In cookie baking, it is most often used to line baking sheets. Using parchment paper means that you will never have to grease and flour a baking sheet again, and it saves on cleanup, too. Parchment paper commonly comes in rolls, but it is very difficult to uncurl. (If you are stuck with this kind of parchment, place a dab of butter in the corner of the baking sheet to glue the paper in place.) With a little searching online, you can find flat sheets of parchment paper cut to fit half-sheet pans, which eliminates the curling problem. Boxed sheets of parchment paper cut to fit full-sheet pans are sold at restaurant suppliers. I shared the expense of a box with other home bakers, and now we all have (close to) lifetime supplies. (The large sheets need to be cut in half to fit the common half-sheet, which is a fair trade-off for the convenience of flat parchment paper.)

SILICONE BAKING MATS, sold under such brand names as Silpat and Expat, are popular with some bakers. They have the same nonstick properties as parchment paper, and can be reused many hundreds of times. Personally, I still prefer baking parchment because my baking mats have been known to pick up other flavors and aromas (such as butter, left from baked cookies on the mats, that has turned rancid). Also, they tend to insulate the cookies, and the bottoms won't crisp as well as those baked on parchment.

Do not substitute wax paper for parchment paper to line cookie sheets. Parchment paper is heatproof to about 400°F (some brands can withstand higher temperatures), but the wax on the wax paper will start to melt at temperatures much lower than that. (It is safe to line cake pans with wax paper, as the batter will cover the paper and protect it from the heat.)

You'll also want a collection of COOKIE CUTTERS to give creative shapes to your cookies. If the box of cookie cutters in my basement is any indication, they can become a minor obsession with bakers. Be sure that the cookie edges are relatively sharp—file them with a knife-sharpening steel if they are dull. Stainless steel or copper cutters keep their edge longer than plastic cutters. Wash the cutters and dry them well before storing.

A PASTRY BAG is needed to shape the *macarons* and meringues on pages 112 and 142. The pastry bag should be at least 12 inches long to hold a sufficient amount of meringue. I use only three ½-INCH-WIDE PASTRY TIPS in this book: plain (Ateco #805), open star (Ateco #825), and French star (Ateco #865). Ateco tips are available at kitchenware shops and online at www.pastrysampler.com.

TECHNIQUES ❧

Most cookies are prepared with the same technique used for making butter cakes—cream the butter and sugar, add the eggs, and then add the flour and leavenings. There are exceptions, as meringue-based cookies seem to be making a good showing in tearooms around the world.

PREPARATIONS

To keep the cookies at a safe distance from the heat source and avoid overbrowning them, position the oven racks in the center and upper third of the oven. (In gas ovens, the heat source is underneath the oven bottom, so placing the rack in the bottom third can easily cause overbrowning.)

Preheat the oven thoroughly before putting in the baking sheets. In most ovens, this takes 15 to 20 minutes, which is a fine time to gather the ingredients and mix the dough. However, take note if the dough needs to be chilled before using, as there is no use preheating an oven if the dough won't be used for a few hours.

Use an oven thermometer to check the oven's accuracy. Alcohol-filled thermometers are more accurate than spring-activated ones. Place the thermometer in the center of the middle rack for the most accurate reading. If the thermometer is too close to the sides of the oven, the reading could be hotter than the actual temperature.

Be sure that all of the ingredients are at room temperature. If necessary, warm the eggs or milk in a bowl of hot water, and soften the butter to the proper malleable consistency.

Line the baking sheets with parchment paper. In most cases, you will only need two baking sheets for an entire batch of cookies.

Sift the dry ingredients together as instructed. This easy step combines and aerates the ingredients so they are easier to mix into the batter. For the many recipes that use baking soda, which tends to clump, sifting pulverizes the leavening and distributes it well. For years, I thought it was sufficient to merely whisk the dry ingredients together, but I also had more than my share of cakes with little pellets of baking soda running through them. Sift the dry ingredients onto a large sheet of parchment or wax paper. When the time comes, use the parchment to lift the ingredients and pour them into the batter.

MIXING COOKIE DOUGH

While there are similarities between mixing the batter for butter cakes and the dough for cookies, there is one major difference. With a cake, the goal is to create as many air bubbles as possible into the batter. With cookies, too many bubbles can create a soufflé effect, making cookies that rise in the oven and then fall during cooling. Usually, 3 minutes is sufficient for creaming butter and sugar for cookies.

Place the room-temperature butter in the bowl of a standing electric mixer fitted with the paddle blade. Beat at high speed until the butter is creamy and looks a shade paler, about 1 minute. At a steady pace (not too slowly), gradually beat in the sugar, about a tablespoon or so at a time, then continue beating until the butter and sugar are homogenous, very pale yellow, and light in texture, about 2 minutes longer. Occasionally stop the mixer to scrape down the sides of the bowl with a rubber spatula. You can cream the butter and sugar in a medium mixing bowl with a hand mixer at high speed, if you wish. And, of course, generations of home-baked cookies before the advent of the electric mixer proved that a wooden spoon and lots of elbow grease can also do the trick.

Now it's time to add the eggs. A familiar phrase in recipes occurs when adding the eggs to the dough, "one at a time, beating well after each addition." If the eggs are added too quickly though, the dough (which is really an emulsified mixture with a careful balance of ingredients) will curdle. Even a single egg, which may not seem like such a large amount of liquid, can be enough to curdle a dough. Sometimes the curdling is corrected when the flour is added, but more often than not, it isn't, and the result is tough cookies. Adding room-temperature, beaten eggs to the batter is the best insurance against curdling. Beat the eggs together in a small bowl until well combined. With the mixer set on medium-high to high speed, add the beaten eggs slowly to the butter-and-sugar mixture, about a tablespoon at a time, so that the emulsification will remain in check. Like the advice for sifting dry ingredients together, this little tip will immensely improve your cookies.

You are now ready to add the dry ingredients (the flour sifted with the leavening, salt, and possibly spices) to the mixture. If you have a standing mixer, the motor will be strong enough to add the dry ingredients. Just be sure to reduce the mixer speed to low, and add the flour mixture gradually to the bowl. If you are using a hand mixer, it may not be strong enough to mix in the flour without straining. In this case, stop the mixer and use a wooden spoon to gradually mix in the flour. When the dough is cohesive, add ingredients such as nuts, dried fruit, or chocolate chips.

Sticky or soft doughs are often refrigerated to make them easier to handle. Just cover the dough in the bowl with plastic wrap and refrigerate it for an hour or so until it is chilled. Do not rush the procedure in the freezer. The edges will harden and freeze before the center chills.

SHAPING COOKIES

Three of the most common types of cookies are identified by the way they are shaped—drop, bar, and rolled cookies.

DROP COOKIES are the easiest to make—just drop the dough from a tablespoon onto the baking sheet. But to create uniformly shaped cookies that will bake at the same rate, you must add a few more moves.

Using a measuring tablespoon, spring-loaded ice-cream scoop, or cookie dough scoop with a 1-tablespoon capacity, scoop up the dough and transfer the roughly shaped "drops" to an unlined baking sheet. After portioning all of the dough, roll each drop between your palms into a ball. Place the balls on another, parchment paper–lined baking sheet, spacing the balls as the recipe directs, but at least 1 inch apart. Some doughs spread more than others and require more distant spacing. If you have any worries that the cookies will spread too much and run into one another, bake a trial cookie or two.

BAR COOKIES are baked as a single unit in a square or oblong pan and cut into individual bars. Even experienced bakers have had grief digging out that first bar, which always crumbles. To solve the problem, line the pan with a "sling" of aluminum foil. This allows the pastry to be completely lifted out of the pan before cutting so you won't have to dig to get the first bar. Tear off a length of aluminum foil (preferably nonstick) about 10 inches longer than the length of the pan. Pleat the foil lengthwise to make a strip of foil equal to the width of the pan. Butter the pan (this helps keep the foil in place) and fit the foil into the pan with the excess foil hanging over the two short sides of the pan. Fold the excess foil down to create "handles." Butter the foil again, even if it is nonstick. If the recipe directs, dust the foil with flour and tap out the excess flour. When the pastry is baked, let it cool in the pan on a wire cake rack. To remove the pastry, run a knife around the inside of the pan to release the pastry from the sides. Lift up the foil handles to remove the pastry in one piece. Place on a cutting board, peel back the foil, and cut into bars with a sharp knife. Remove the bars from the foil.

The dough for ROLLED COOKIES is rolled out and cut into decorative shapes. Be sure that the dough is chilled first, but it will be easiest to work with if it is merely cold and not refrigerated until it is rock hard. An hour or two in the refrigerator is usually sufficient. Do not freeze the dough to speed the chilling. If the dough is too hard, it will crack when rolled. In that case, let it stand at room temperature for a few minutes to warm slightly.

Dust a work surface with flour. Place the unwrapped dough on the work surface and dust the top of the dough with flour. Using a rolling pin (a nonstick silicone pin works best), roll out the dough about ⅛ inch thick (or a little thicker for softer, more substantial cookies), occasionally slipping a long metal icing spatula under the dough to be sure that it isn't sticking. Using a cookie cutter, cut out the cookies. You may need to slide the spatula under the cookies to move them. Transfer to the parchment paper–lined baking sheets, spacing at least 1 inch apart. Sugar cookies will not spread much, unless the dough is warm. (If you think the dough has softened, refrigerate the cookies on the baking sheet for a few minutes before baking—in cold weather, place near an open window or on a screened porch.) Gather up the dough scraps, press them into a thick disk, and wrap and refrigerate the disk for 5 to 10 minutes before rolling out the rest of the cookies.

You'll find complete instructions for shaping specialty cookies, such as *macarons* and madeleines, in their recipes.

BAKING AND COOLING

The oven racks should be positioned in the center and upper third of the oven before preheating. Providing two oven rack positions is a matter of convenience for the home baker to speed up the baking process. You will have much more control over the baking if you only use the center rack. However, if you stay aware (and use a kitchen timer), you can use two racks at once, as long as you move the positions of the baking sheets halfway during the baking time. Switch the baking sheets from top to bottom, and turn them from front to back. Always bake bar cookies in the center rack.

If you need to reuse the baking sheets to bake more cookies, be sure that the baking sheets are cool before placing the dough on them. If the dough comes into contact with a warm baking sheet, it will spread, and the cookies will be flat.

In most cases, the cookies can be allowed to cool on their baking sheets with no harm done. But they will cool more quickly (and free up the sheets for the next batch) if they are transferred to a wire cake rack. Let the cookies cool on the baking sheet for a few minutes before moving them to the rack.

STORING

Even the most adorable cookie jar isn't a good place to keep cookies, which need airtight storage to stave off staling. Metal and plastic containers are excellent choices; just separate the layers of cookies with wax paper. Try to store each type of cookie in its own container, as mixing up varieties can affect their textures. For example, if stored together, moisture from a bar cookie can soften a crisp drop cookie.

FROM THE COOKIE JAR

Here are treats from the American cookie canon, with familiar and comforting flavors. They are the kind of old-fashioned cookies that you might serve to close friends who have dropped in for a spot of tea. But you'll also find some surprising twists on old favorites.

❦ BLACK-AND-WHITE COOKIES

Black-and-white cookies are a New York specialty that you will find at every delicatessen. *Seinfeld* fans will remember them from "The Dinner Party." They are not quite cookies, but saucer-size disks of cake (urban legend says that they were originally created to use up leftover cake batter), with very dark brown and white icing applied on the flat side. Make them for transplanted New Yorkers, and they will be forever grateful.

BLACK-AND-WHITE COOKIES

2½ cups all-purpose flour

2½ cups cake flour (not self-rising)

1 teaspoon baking powder

½ teaspoon salt

1 cup whole milk

1 teaspoon vanilla extract

½ teaspoon lemon extract

1 cup (2 sticks) unsalted butter, at room temperature

1¾ cups granulated sugar

4 large eggs, beaten, at room temperature

ICINGS

7½ cups (about 1½ pounds) confectioners' sugar

¼ cup light corn syrup

1 teaspoon vanilla extract (preferably clear, available at crafts stores)

¼ cup Dutch-processed cocoa powder

White icing coloring, optional (see Note)

1. Position racks in the top third and center of the oven and preheat to 375°F. Cut 6 sheets of parchment paper to fit large baking sheets. Using a 4½-inch-diameter saucer or bowl as a template, draw 4 rounds spaced at least 1½ inches apart on each sheet of paper. Turn the paper upside down (you should be able to see the rounds through the paper) and line two large baking sheets with the paper.

2. To make the cookies, sift the flours, baking powder, and salt together. Mix the milk, vanilla, and lemon extract together. Cream the butter in a large bowl with an electric mixer set on high speed until smooth, about 1 minute. Gradually beat in the granulated sugar and continue beating until the mixture is very light in color and texture, about 3 minutes. Gradually beat in the eggs. Reduce the mixer speed to low. In thirds, alternating with two equal additions of the milk mixture, beat in the flour mixture, scraping down the sides of the bowl often with a rubber spatula, and mix just until smooth.

3. Using an ice-cream scoop with about ¼ cup capacity, transfer portions of batter to the centers of the rounds on the baking sheet. Using a small offset metal spatula or the back of a spoon, and using the template on the paper as a guide, spread the batter into 4½-inch rounds.

4. Bake, switching the position of the baking sheets from top to bottom and front to back halfway through baking, until the edges of the cookies are beginning to brown and the tops of the cookies spring back when gently pressed in the centers, 12 to 14 minutes. Let cool for 5 minutes on the baking sheets. Transfer to wire cake racks and cool completely. Repeat with the remaining parchment paper, being sure to use cooled baking sheets. (If necessary to cool them quickly, rinse the baking sheets under cold water and dry.)

5. To make the icings, sift the confectioners' sugar into a large bowl. Bring the corn syrup and ⅔ cup of water to a boil in a small saucepan over medium heat. Pour over the sugar, add the vanilla, and whisk until smooth to make an icing that is a little thicker than heavy cream. Adjust the consistency by adding water, a teaspoon at a time, if necessary.

6. Transfer 1 cup of the icing to a heatproof medium bowl. Add the cocoa and whisk until smooth, adjusting the icing to its original consistency with teaspoons of water. Place the bowl in a skillet of very hot water over very low heat to keep the chocolate icing from setting.

7. Add enough white icing coloring, if using, to the plain icing to give it an opaque sheen. Brush away any loose crumbs from the flat side of the cookie with a pastry brush. Using a small offset spatula, spread the white icing on half of the flat underside of each cookie. Let stand until the icing is set, about 10 minutes. The icing on the cookie should be opaque as possible, so apply a second coating, if you wish.

8. Whisk the chocolate icing to dissolve any crust on its surface. Remove the bowl from the skillet. Spread the empty flat side of each cookie with the chocolate icing. Let stand until the icing is completely set, at least 1 hour. (The cookies can be made up to 3 days ahead, stored in a large airtight container and separated by sheets of wax paper.)

NOTE: The white icing should be as white and opaque as possible, and adding white icing coloring will help accomplish this. Look for Wilton's White-White Icing Coloring or Spectrum Bright White at cake decorating and hobby shops (see Sources). If you don't use the coloring, you may need to apply a second layer of icing over the first one to completely mask the cookies. Or don't bother with the coloring, as the icing will not be opaque, but it will still be delicious.

BROWNIE BITES ❧

In the world of cookies, brownies are surely on the short list of absolute favorites. And while there are different styles of brownies, I like them moist, chewy, and fudgy. Here they are, dressed up in minimalist chic—cut into cubes and cloaked in dark chocolate to make small, intensely flavored bites. Use your favorite eating chocolate for the ganache, but keep in mind that the ganache may curdle if the cacao content of your chosen chocolate is higher than 62 percent, so check the label. (If there is no percentage listed, the chocolate is probably fine to use for ganache.) For an especially pretty look appropriate for a high tea, top each square with an unsprayed edible flower blossom, such as johnny-jump-ups or a small rose petal. If you are a fan of chocolate-flavored tea, serve it with these for a doubly chocolate tea experience.

BROWNIES

Softened butter for the pan

½ cup all-purpose flour, plus more for the pan

¼ teaspoon baking soda

¼ teaspoon salt

6 tablespoons (¾ stick) unsalted butter, cut up

3 ounces unsweetened chocolate, finely chopped

½ cup granulated sugar

½ cup packed light brown sugar

2 large eggs, beaten, at room temperature

2 tablespoons light corn syrup

1 teaspoon vanilla extract

GANACHE

1 cup heavy cream

8 ounces finely chopped semisweet or bittersweet chocolate (no higher than 62 percent cacao content)

1. Position a rack in the center of the oven and preheat to 350°F. Lightly butter the inside of an 11½ x 8-inch baking pan. Line the bottom of the pan with wax paper. Dust the inside of the pan with flour and tap out the excess.

2. To make the brownies, sift the flour, baking soda, and salt together. Melt the butter in a medium saucepan over medium-low heat. Remove from the heat and add the chocolate. Let stand until the chocolate softens, about 3 minutes. Whisk until smooth. Whisk in the sugars, then gradually whisk in the eggs, then the corn syrup and vanilla. Stir in the flour mixture, just until smooth. Spread evenly in the baking pan.

3. Bake until a wooden toothpick inserted in the center of the brownie comes out with a moist crumb, about 25 minutes. Let cool completely in the pan on a wire cake rack.

4. Invert the brownie onto a cutting board and remove the wax paper. Use a sharp, thin-bladed knife to cut the brownie vertically into 6 rows, then horizontally into 5 rows, to make 30 pieces. If you wish, trim any raised edges to give the brownies a tailored appearance. (Freeze the brownie trimmings to sprinkle on ice cream.)

5. To make the ganache, bring the cream to a simmer over medium heat. Remove from the heat and add the chocolate. Let stand until the chocolate melts, about 3 minutes. Stir with a rubber spatula until smooth. (Whisking could create bubbles that will mar the surface of the icing.)

6. Arrange the brownies, smooth bottoms up, on a wire cake rack set over a rimmed baking sheet. Working with a few pieces at a time, spoon the warm ganache over each brownie. Use a small offset metal spatula to smooth the ganache over the top of each brownie, letting the excess ganache run down the sides. Do not cover the sides of the brownies completely, as the bare portions will make the brownies easier to pick up. Let stand until the ganache is set, about 1 hour. (The brownies can be made up to 3 days ahead, covered and stored at room temperature.)

CHERRY AND WHITE CHIP COOKIES ❧

If you are looking for kid-friendly cookies (say, for a young girl's first tea party), these are a good bet. Grown-ups will find that the fruit and vanilla flavors in these chewy cookies are made for a hot cup of black tea. For plump cookies that won't deflate when they come out of the oven (a common problem with chocolate chip cookies), do not overcream the butter and sugar. Also, chill the dough before shaping the cookies. These two little secrets will forever change the way you make chocolate chip cookies.

2¼ cups all-purpose flour

1 teaspoon baking soda

½ teaspoon salt

1 cup (2 sticks) unsalted butter, at room temperature

⅔ cup granulated sugar

⅔ cup packed light brown sugar

1 large egg plus 1 large egg yolk, beaten together

2 tablespoons light corn syrup, golden syrup, or honey

2 teaspoons vanilla extract

1 cup white chocolate chips

1 cup dried tart or sweet cherries

1. Sift the flour, baking soda, and salt together. Beat the butter and the granulated and brown sugars together in a medium bowl with an electric mixer on high speed just until the mixture turns pale, about 2 minutes. Do not overbeat. Gradually beat in the egg mixture, then the corn syrup and vanilla. Gradually stir in the flour mixture to make a stiff dough. Stir in the white chocolate chips and dried cherries. Cover the bowl and refrigerate until chilled, about 1½ hours. Do not chill for more than 2 hours, or the baking soda may lose its strength.

2. Position racks in the center and upper third of the oven and preheat to 350°F. Line two large baking sheets with parchment paper.

3. Using a rounded tablespoon for each, drop the dough onto the baking sheets, spacing them 1 inch apart. Bake, switching the position of the baking sheets from top to bottom and front to back halfway through baking, until the cookies are golden brown around the edges, about 10 minutes. Let cool on the pans for 3 minutes. Transfer the cookies to wire cake racks and cool completely. (The cookies can be stored at room temperature in an airtight container for up to 2 days.)

CHEWY GINGER COOKIES

My friend Arlene Stein, executive assistant to Sarabeth Levine of Sarabeth's Bakery, shared her ginger cookie recipe with me, promising that it was a special one. As Arlene is exposed to a lot of great baking, I knew that she knows her cookies and wouldn't exaggerate. Fresh ginger gives them a rich spiciness, and coarse sugar provides a nice, slightly crunchy exterior. Best of all, when baked just right, they turn out comfortingly chewy. If they are a tad overbaked, don't worry—they will be crisp and more like gingersnaps. So, if the chewiness is important to you, do a test batch for timing. And note that the dough needs a few hours of refrigeration before baking. Make Gingered Green Tea (page 31) to serve with these.

2¼ cups all-purpose flour

½ teaspoon baking powder

½ teaspoon baking soda

½ teaspoon salt

1 cup granulated sugar

12 tablespoons (1½ sticks) unsalted butter, at room temperature

3 tablespoons peeled and grated fresh ginger (use the medium-size holes on a box grater)

¼ cup unsulfured molasses

1 large egg, at room temperature

½ cup turbinado, raw, or additional granulated sugar for coating the cookies

1. Sift the flour, baking powder, baking soda, and salt together. Beat the granulated sugar and butter together in a medium bowl with an electric mixer at high speed, occasionally scraping down the sides of the bowl, just until the mixture is light in color, about 2 minutes. Do not overbeat. Beat in the ginger, then the molasses and egg, scraping down the sides of the bowl as needed. Gradually stir in the flour mixture to make a soft dough.

2. Cover the bowl with plastic wrap. Refrigerate until the dough is chilled and firm, at least 3 hours or overnight.

3. Position racks in the top third and center of the oven and preheat to 350°F. Line two large baking sheets with parchment paper.

4. Using a scant tablespoon for each cookie, roll the dough into balls. Roll each in the turbinado sugar to coat. Place the balls 2 inches apart on the baking sheets.

5. Bake, switching the position of the baking sheets from top to bottom and front to back halfway through baking, until the edges of the cookies are set and dry, but the interiors seem slightly underdone, about 12 minutes. Let cool on the pans for 5 minutes. Transfer the cookies to wire cake racks and let cool completely. (The cookies can be made up to 1 week ahead, stored in an airtight container at room temperature.)

❧ OATMEAL COOKIES WITH MILK CHOCOLATE AND RAISINS

MAKES 4½ DOZEN COOKIES

Looking for a way to jazz up an old favorite, I tossed some chocolate-covered raisins in my oatmeal cookie dough, but because the thin chocolate shells were not formulated for baking, the results were less than stellar. On my next try I used milk chocolate chips and raisins, and success was mine. For plump, chewy cookies refrigerate the dough for about an hour before shaping—freshly made dough tends to spread in the heat of the oven.

3½ cups rolled (old-fashioned) oats

1½ cups all-purpose flour

1 teaspoon baking soda

1 teaspoon baking powder

½ teaspoon salt

1 cup (2 sticks) unsalted butter, at room temperature

1 cup granulated sugar

1 cup packed light brown sugar

2 large eggs, at room temperature, beaten

2 teaspoons vanilla extract

1 cup seedless raisins

1 cup milk chocolate chips or chunks

1. Grind ½ cup of the oats in a food processor fitted with a metal chopping blade until powdery. Add the flour, baking soda, baking powder, and salt and pulse until combined. Pour into a bowl, add the remaining 3 cups oats, and stir until mixed together.

2. Cream the butter and sugars together in a large bowl with an electric mixer on high speed, occasionally scraping down the sides of the bowl, just until the mixture is light in color, about 2 minutes. Gradually beat in the eggs, then the vanilla. Gradually stir in the flour mixture. Stir in the raisins and milk chocolate chips. Cover the bowl and refrigerate to chill lightly, 1 to 2 hours.

3. Position racks in the top third and center of the oven and preheat to 350°F. Line two large baking sheets with parchment paper.

4. Using a tablespoon for each cookie, shape the dough into 1-inch balls. Place 2 inches apart on the baking sheets. Bake, switching the position of the baking sheets from top to bottom and front to back halfway through baking, until the edges of the cookies are light golden brown, 12 to 14 minutes.

5. Let cool on the baking sheets for 5 minutes. Transfer to wire cake racks and let cool completely. Repeat with the remaining dough, using cooled baking sheets. (The cookies can be stored in an airtight container at room temperature for up to 5 days.)

✿ HONEY NUT DROPS

MAKES 2½ DOZEN COOKIES

If you like to sweeten your tea with honey, you will love these. With their homey appearance, they may not be the prettiest cookies on the tea tray, but their honeyed sweetness will make them a favorite. Honey is a humectant, which means that it absorbs moisture from the ambient atmosphere, so the drops will stay moist for days, making them an especially good choice for when you need to make cookies well ahead of serving.

1⅓ cups all-purpose flour

1 teaspoon baking powder

½ teaspoon baking soda

½ teaspoon salt

6 tablespoons (¾ stick) unsalted butter, at room temperature

½ cup mild-flavored honey, such as orange blossom (see Note)

1 large egg, at room temperature

1 teaspoon vanilla extract

¾ cup coarsely chopped walnuts

1. Position a rack in the top third and center of the oven and preheat to 350°F. Line two baking sheets with parchment paper.

2. Sift together the flour, baking powder, baking soda, and salt. Cream the butter and honey together in a medium bowl with an electric mixer on high speed until the mixture is light in color and texture, about 3 minutes. Beat in the egg, then the vanilla. Gradually stir in the flour mixture and mix just until the dough is combined. Stir in the walnuts.

3. Using a scant tablespoon for each cookie, shape the dough into 1-inch balls. Place 1½ inches apart on the baking sheets. Bake, switching the position of the baking sheets

from top to bottom and front to back halfway through baking, until the cookies are light golden brown on the bottom, 12 to 15 minutes.

4. Let cool on the sheets for 5 minutes. Transfer to wire cake racks and cool completely. (The cookies can be made up to 5 days ahead, stored in airtight containers at room temperature.)

NOTE: For baking, use a mildly flavored honey. A moderately priced supermarket brand, usually blended from a variety of honeys to give consistent product, is fine. Honeys with distinctive flavors, such as sage, lavender, or chestnut, tend to intensify when heated, and the strong taste isn't always welcome.

❧ CHAI SNICKERDOODLES

Snickerdoodles are one of the great American cookies, and there are many stories about how they got their whimsical name. They may be common, but they are one of my favorite teatime treats, as their spiciness is a great pairing with black tea or chai. While they are usually spiced with just cinnamon, my version adds other warm spices that you are likely to find in chai to give them a makeover. If you like these chewy (as I do), bake them at the low end of the baking time, or bake at the high end of the range for crisp cookies.

2¼ cups all-purpose flour

1 tablespoon baking powder

¾ teaspoon ground cinnamon, divided

¼ teaspoon ground cardamom (see Note)

¼ teaspoon freshly grated nutmeg

⅛ teaspoon ground cloves

1 cup (2 sticks) unsalted butter, at room temperature

1¾ cups sugar, divided

2 large eggs, beaten, at room temperature

1. Position a rack in the top third and center of the oven and preheat to 350°F. Line two large baking sheets with parchment paper.

2. Sift the flour, baking powder, ½ teaspoon of the cinnamon, cardamom, nutmeg, and cloves together. Cream the butter in a medium bowl with an electric mixer on high speed until creamy, about 1 minute. Gradually beat in 1½ cups of the sugar and beat until the mixture is light in color and texture, about 2 minutes. Do not overbeat. Gradually beat in the eggs. Gradually stir in the flour mixture.

3. Combine the remaining ¼ cup sugar and ¼ teaspoon cinnamon in a small bowl. Using a scant tablespoon for each cookie, shape the dough into 1-inch balls. Roll in the sugar mixture to coat. Place 2 inches apart on the baking sheets. Bake, switching the position of the baking sheets from top to bottom and front to back halfway through baking, until the edges of the cookies are light golden brown, 12 to 14 minutes. (For crisper cookies, bake until the tops are beginning to brown, about 16 minutes.) The cookies will be puffed, but they will deflate and have crackled tops when cooled.

4. Let cool on the baking sheets for 5 minutes. Transfer to wire cake racks and let cool completely. (The cookies can be stored in an airtight container at room temperature for up to 5 days.)

NOTE: Remove the seeds from cardamom pods, and grind the seeds in an electric spice grinder or with a mortar and pestle. The flavor will be fresher than preground cardamom in a jar. You'll find reasonably priced cardamom pods at Indian grocers.

BAR COOKIES

Chunky bar cookies, which are typically eaten with your fingers, add a casual, friendly note to a selection of tea cookies. They can be homey (as with the moist-and-chewy Granola Bars), creamy (Blueberry Cheesecake Bars), or elegant (Linzer Squares, with a hazelnut crust and raspberry filling).

BLUEBERRY CHEESECAKE BARS

Cool, creamy, and bursting with blueberries, these bars are perfect for summertime entertaining. For a smooth, lump-free filling, have all of the ingredients at room temperature, as the cream cheese will firm up if it comes into contact with a cold egg or sour cream. Be sure that the cream cheese is well softened—let it stand at room temperature for at least 2 hours before mixing. And keep in mind that frozen berries will chill the filling batter, and so if they are used, add a few minutes to the baking time. Make these bars with the classic graham cracker crust, or crush store-bought gingersnap cookies into crumbs and use them as a variation.

CRUST

Softened unsalted butter for the pan

1 cup well-crushed graham crackers or gingersnaps

1 tablespoon sugar

4 tablespoons (½ stick) unsalted butter, melted

FILLING

8 ounces cream cheese, well softened at room temperature

½ cup sugar

1 large egg, at room temperature

3 tablespoons sour cream, at room temperature

Grated zest of ½ orange or 1 lemon

½ teaspoon vanilla extract

1 cup fresh or frozen blueberries

1. Position a rack in the center of the oven and preheat to 350°F. Lightly butter the inside of an 8-inch square baking pan. Pleat a 17-inch-long piece of aluminum foil (preferably nonstick) lengthwise to an 8-inch width. Place in the pan, lining the bottom and two

of the sides with the foil, letting the excess foil hang over the sides to act as "handles." Butter the foil, even if it is nonstick.

2. To make the crust, combine the crumbs and sugar in a medium bowl. Add the butter and stir until moistened. Press the crumbs firmly and evenly into the bottom of the pan. Bake until the crumbs are set and give off a toasty aroma, about 12 minutes. Remove from the oven.

3. Meanwhile, make the filling. Mix the cream cheese in a medium bowl with an electric mixer on medium speed just until smooth. Gradually beat in the sugar, scraping down the sides of the bowl often, then beat in the egg. Add the sour cream, zest, and vanilla and mix just until combined. Stir in the blueberries. Spread over the crust in the pan.

4. Bake until the filling moves as a unit when the pan is lightly shaken (the center may seem slightly unset) and the edges are slightly puffed and barely beginning to brown, 25 to 30 minutes.

5. Transfer to a wire cake rack and let cool completely in the pan. Cover the pan with plastic wrap and refrigerate until chilled, at least 4 hours or overnight.

6. Run a knife around the inside edge of the pan to loosen the cheesecake from the sides. Lift up on the foil handles to remove the cheesecake in one piece. Peel back the foil on the sides. Using a thin, sharp knife dipped into hot water, cut the cheesecake into 16 bars. (The cheesecake bars can be stored, covered in plastic wrap and refrigerated, for up to 2 days.) Serve chilled.

CASHEW BLONDIES

Vanilla lovers unite! As much as I enjoy dark chocolate with my tea, sometimes I'm in the mood for one of these chewy butterscotch bars. Cashews, with underlying notes of both vanilla and butter, are the nuts to use here. To complement the blondies' caramel notes, sweeten your favorite black tea with demerara or muscovado sugar.

Softened butter for the pan

2¼ cups all-purpose flour, plus more for the pan

1½ teaspoons baking powder

½ teaspoon baking soda

¼ teaspoon salt

12 tablespoons (1½ sticks) unsalted butter, cut up

1¾ cups packed light or dark brown sugar

3 large eggs, beaten

1½ teaspoons vanilla extract

2 cups (8 ounces) roasted unsalted cashews, 1½ cups coarsely chopped and ½ cup finely chopped

3 ounces white chocolate, finely chopped

1. Position a rack in the center of the oven and preheat to 350°F. Butter a 9 x 13-inch metal baking pan. Pleat a 23-inch-long piece of aluminum foil (preferably nonstick) lengthwise to a 9-inch width. Place in the pan, lining the bottom and the two short sides with the foil, letting the excess foil hang over the sides to act as "handles." If the foil is not nonstick, lightly butter the foil. Dust the inside of the pan with flour and tap out the excess.

2. Sift the flour, baking powder, baking soda, and salt together. Melt the butter in a medium saucepan over medium heat. Remove from the heat. Add the brown sugar and stir until smooth. Gradually stir in the eggs, then the vanilla. Add the flour mixture and stir until smooth. Fold in the coarsely chopped cashews. Spread evenly in the pan.

3. Bake until a wooden toothpick inserted in the center of the blondie comes out clean, about 25 minutes. Transfer to a wire cake rack and let cool in the pan.

4. Melt the white chocolate in the top part of a double boiler over hot, not simmering, water. Remove from the heat.

5. Run a knife around the inside edge of the pan to loosen the blondie from the sides. Lift up on the foil handles to remove it from the pan in one piece. Drizzle the white chocolate over the top. Sprinkle with the finely chopped cashews. Let stand until the white chocolate is set. Cut into 30 bars. (The blondies can be stored in an airtight container at room temperature for up to 5 days.)

GRANOLA BARS ✲

These moist bars include some of the familiar ingredients of granola, including oats, brown sugar, coconut, and nuts. I like raspberry preserves as the filling, but you can use your favorite—apricot or strawberry are nice, too. Leftovers from your tea party will make excellent additions to a lunch box.

Softened butter for the pan (optional)

2½ cups all-purpose flour

1 teaspoon baking soda

½ teaspoon salt

2 cups rolled (old-fashioned) oats

1 cup sweetened coconut flakes

½ cup finely chopped walnuts

1 cup (2 sticks) unsalted butter, at room temperature

2 cups packed light brown sugar

2 large eggs, beaten, at room temperature

1½ teaspoons vanilla extract

1 cup raspberry preserves

1. Position a rack in the center of the oven and preheat to 350°F. Lightly butter a 9 x 13-inch baking pan. Pleat a 23-inch-long piece of aluminum foil (preferably non-stick) lengthwise to a 9-inch width. Place in the pan, lining the bottom and the two short sides with the foil, letting the excess foil hang over the sides to act as "handles." If the foil is not nonstick, lightly butter the foil.

2. Sift the flour, baking soda, and salt together into a medium bowl. Add the oats, coconut, and walnuts and stir well.

3. Beat the butter in a medium bowl with an electric mixer on high speed until the butter is creamy, about 1 minute. Gradually beat in the brown sugar and beat until the

mixture is light in color and texture, about 3 minutes. Gradually beat in the eggs, then the vanilla. Gradually stir in the flour mixture. Reserve 2 cups of the dough. Press the remaining dough into the pan. Dollop the preserves over the surface of the dough in the pan, then spread evenly with a metal spatula. Crumble the reserved dough as evenly as possible over the preserves.

4. Bake until the top of the pastry is lightly browned and the preserves are bubbling, 30 to 35 minutes. Transfer the pan to a wire cake rack. Let cool completely in the pan.

5. Lift up on the foil handles to remove the pastry in one piece. Cut into 30 bars. (The bars can be stored in an airtight container at room temperature for up to 3 days.)

LEMON RASPBERRY SQUARES

MAKES 16 BARS

There are countless lemon square recipes out there, but I want to encourage you to try these, made a tad more puckery with the addition of red raspberries. The berries give these a festive touch that is welcome at a special tea. Blueberries are an excellent alternative to the raspberries, or use a combination of berries, adding a few blackberries to the mix. And I highly recommend the passion fruit variation.

CRUST

5 tablespoons unsalted butter, cut into tablespoons, at room temperature, plus more for the pan

1 cup all-purpose flour, plus more for the pan

2 tablespoons confectioners' sugar

Pinch of salt

FILLING

1½ cups granulated sugar

1 tablespoon plus 2 teaspoons cornstarch

1 teaspoon baking powder

¼ teaspoon salt

4 large eggs

Grated zest of 2 lemons

½ cup fresh lemon juice (about 3 lemons)

One 6-ounce container fresh raspberries

Confectioners' sugar for garnish (optional)

1. Position a rack in the center of the oven and preheat to 350°F. Lightly butter the inside of an 8-inch square baking pan. Pleat a 17-inch-long piece of aluminum foil (preferably nonstick) lengthwise to an 8-inch width. Place in the pan, lining the bottom and two of the sides with the foil, letting the excess foil hang over the sides to act as "handles." Butter the foil, even if it is nonstick. Dust the inside of the pan with flour and tap out the excess.

2. To make the crust, pulse the flour, confectioners' sugar, and salt in a food processor fitted with the metal blade to combine. Add the butter and pulse about 15 times, or until the mixture starts to clump together. Press the dough firmly and evenly into the baking pan. Pierce the dough all over with a fork.

3. Bake until the crust is set and beginning to brown around the edges, about 12 minutes. Remove from the oven.

4. To make the filling, whisk the granulated sugar, cornstarch, baking powder, and salt together in a medium bowl. Add the eggs and lemon zest and whisk until combined. Gradually whisk in the lemon juice.

5. Spread the raspberries evenly over the crust. Pour in the filling. Bake until the filling is puffed and golden brown, about 30 minutes.

6. Transfer to a wire cake rack and let cool in the pan. Run a sharp knife around the inside edge of the pan to loosen the pastry. Lift up on the foil handles to remove the pastry in one piece. Using a sharp knife, cut into 16 squares. Sift confectioners' sugar, if using, over the squares and serve. (The lemon squares can be refrigerated in an airtight container for up to 3 days.)

PASSION FRUIT SQUARES: These are sensational, if you have access to frozen passion fruit pulp. It isn't practical to use fresh passion fruit as they are prohibitively expensive, and each fruit yields only about 1 tablespoon of pulp. (For this recipe, you would need at least 10 passion fruits.) Instead of the lemon juice and zest, substitute 2/3 cup thawed frozen passion fruit pulp, available in the frozen section of Latino supermarkets. Omit the raspberries.

❧ LINZER SQUARES

For centuries, the Austrian city of Linz has been famous for Linzertorte, a kind of jam tart with a crust redolent of warm spices and roasted nuts. The concept takes well to a cookie treatment, yielding tender, fruit-filled squares whose spiciness is perfect with a cup of tea. For the filling, use regular preserves, as they have a firmer consistency than the seedless variety, and rub them through a sieve to remove the seeds, if you wish. Try to make these a day ahead to mellow the flavors and soften the crust. Chai may seem like an odd match for these cookies, but the spices in each complement the other well. Serve the one on page 32, or your favorite.

Softened butter for the pan

¾ cup hazelnuts, toasted and skinned (see Note)

¾ cup sugar

1½ cups all-purpose flour

2 teaspoons Dutch-processed or natural cocoa powder

½ teaspoon baking powder

½ teaspoon ground cinnamon

¼ teaspoon ground cloves

¼ teaspoon salt

8 tablespoons (1 stick) cold unsalted butter, cut into ½-inch cubes

1 large egg, beaten

1 teaspoon vanilla extract

Grated zest of ½ lemon

One 12-ounce jar raspberry preserves (not seedless preserves), rubbed through a wire sieve to remove seeds

1. Position a rack in the center of the oven and preheat to 350°F. Lightly butter the inside of an 8-inch square baking pan. Pleat a 17-inch-long piece of aluminum foil (preferably nonstick) lengthwise to an 8-inch width. Place in the pan, lining the bottom and two of the sides with the foil, letting the excess foil hang over the

sides to act as "handles." Butter the foil, even if it is nonstick.

2. Process the hazelnuts and sugar in a food processor until the hazelnuts are very finely ground, almost a powder. Add the flour, cocoa, baking powder, cinnamon, cloves, and salt and pulse to combine. Add the butter and pulse until the mixture resembles coarse meal. Add the egg, vanilla, and lemon zest and pulse until the mixture begins to clump together. Transfer the dough to a lightly floured work surface. Using the heel of your hand, press and smear the dough onto the work surface until it is well combined. Using a bench scraper or a metal spatula, gather up the dough and press into a thick disk.

3. Line a baking sheet with parchment paper. Place half of the dough on the baking sheet, and shape into an 8-inch square, using the bottom of the baking pan as a template. Add any of the trimmings to the remaining dough. Press the remaining dough into the bottom and ⅛ inch up the sides of the prepared pan. Pierce the dough in a few places with a fork. Refrigerate the dough on the baking sheet to chill and firm it while baking the dough in the pan.

4. Bake until the dough is set, about 10 minutes. Remove from the oven. Spread the sieved preserves over the dough in the pan. Remove the dough from the refrigerator. Using a pizza wheel, cut the chilled dough into ¼-inch-thick strips. Arrange the strips in an overlapping diagonal lattice pattern on the preserves, trimming and piecing the strips together as needed. Return to the oven and bake until the dough is very lightly browned and the preserves about 1 inch away from the center of the pan are bubbling, 30 to 35 minutes.

5. Let cool completely in the pan on a wire cake rack. Run a sharp knife around the inside edge of the pan to release the cookie from the sides. Lift up on the handles to remove from the pan in one piece. Peel away the foil. Using a thin, sharp knife, cut into 25 squares. (The cookies are best if stored in an airtight container at room temperature for 1 day before serving. They will keep for up to 5 days, stored in the same manner.)

NOTE: To toast hazelnuts, spread the nuts on a rimmed baking sheet. Bake in a preheated 350°F oven until the skins are cracked and the nut flesh is golden brown, 12 to 15 minutes. Wrap the nuts in a clean kitchen towel and let stand until cool enough to handle. Using the towel, rub the skins off the nuts. Don't worry about removing every last shred of skin.

MAPLE PECAN SQUARES 🎋

Pecan pie is a popular dessert, to be sure, but with corn syrup as the main sweetener, it can easily cross over the line from the merely sugary to the annoyingly cloying. These nutty cookies, which clearly are inspired by pecan pie, are sweetened with pure maple syrup, which makes a big difference. Supermarket-brand maple-flavored pancake syrup—artificially flavored corn syrup and not the real thing—is a barely acceptable substitute.

CRUST

12 tablespoons (1½ sticks) unsalted butter, cut into tablespoons, at room temperature, plus more for the pan

2 cups all-purpose flour

3 tablespoons granulated sugar

¼ teaspoon salt

FILLING

¾ cup maple syrup, preferably Grade B (see Note)

¾ cup packed light brown sugar, rubbed through a sieve to remove lumps

2 large eggs

2 tablespoons unsalted butter, melted

¾ teaspoon vanilla extract

2 cups (8 ounces) chopped pecans

1. Position a rack in the center of the oven and preheat to 350°F. Lightly butter a 13 x 9-inch (quarter-sheet) rimmed baking sheet.

2. To make the crust, pulse the flour, granulated sugar, and salt in a food processor until combined. Add the butter and pulse until the mixture begins to clump together. Press the dough firmly and evenly into the baking sheet. Pierce the dough well with a fork.

3. Bake until the crust is lightly browned, about 25 minutes. Remove the baking sheet from the oven.

4. To make the filling, whisk the maple syrup, brown sugar, eggs, butter, and vanilla until the sugar dissolves. Sprinkle the pecans evenly over the crust, and pour the filling on top. Return to the oven and bake until the filling is set, about 25 minutes.

5. Let cool completely in the pan on a wire cake rack.

6. Cut into 30 bars and serve. (The cookies can be made up to 3 days ahead, stored at room temperature in an airtight container.)

NOTE: The main criterion for grading maple syrup is depth of flavor, and not quality. While Grade A has the most delicate flavor, the full, rich taste of Grade B maple syrup is better for baking. You'll find it at natural food stores and many "club" markets, such as Trader Joe's. If you must use Grade A, expect a gentler maple flavor, or perhaps add ¼ teaspoon maple flavor extract to the filling.

ELEGANT COOKIES FOR TEATIME

For a special occasion, you may want to serve cookies that take a little more attention than usual—cookies with a certain sophistication and finesse. These cookies have been cut, sandwiched, or otherwise molded into delightful shapes with equally delightful flavors.

❧ ALFAJORES

A few years ago, during one of my holiday cooking classes, an Argentine-born student (whose name I unfortunately never got) told me about *alfajores,* meltingly tender cookies sandwiched with rich dulce de leche. The next time she attended class, she brought me the recipe. The cornstarch in the dough gives the cookies their amazing delicate texture. I can't recommend *alfajores* highly enough. The creamy aroma and flavor of Formosa Milk oolong is sensational with the caramel-like dulce de leche.

1¼ cups all-purpose flour	½ cup granulated sugar
¾ cup cornstarch	1 large egg plus 1 egg yolk, beaten together
1 teaspoon baking powder	⅔ cup store-bought dulce de leche (see Note)
¼ teaspoon salt	Confectioners' sugar for garnish (optional)
8 tablespoons (1 stick) unsalted butter, at room temperature	

1. Sift the flour, cornstarch, baking powder, and salt together. Cream the butter and granulated sugar together in a large bowl with an electric mixer on high speed until the mixture is very light in color and texture, about 2 minutes. Do not overbeat. Gradually beat in the egg mixture. Gradually stir in the flour mixture to make a soft dough.

2. Divide the dough in half and shape each portion into a thick disk. Wrap each in plastic wrap or wax paper. Refrigerate until chilled and firm enough to roll out, at least 2 hours and up to 1 day. (If the dough is very chilled and hard, let it stand at room temperature for 10 minutes before rolling out.)

3. Position a rack in the center of the oven and preheat the oven to 350°F. Line two large baking sheets with parchment paper.

4. Unwrap one portion of dough and place on a lightly floured work surface. Dust the top with flour and roll out ⅛ inch thick. Using a 2¼-inch-wide heart-shaped cookie cutter, cut out hearts of dough and transfer them to a baking sheet, placing 1 inch apart. Gather up the scraps and roll out until all of the dough has been cut out. Repeat with the other portion of dough.

5. Bake, switching the position of the baking sheets from top to bottom and front to back halfway through baking, until cookies look set and dry, but are not browned at all, 12 to 14 minutes.

6. Let cool on the baking sheets for 5 minutes. Transfer to wire cake racks and let cool completely.

7. For each cookie, dollop about 1 teaspoon of the dulce de leche onto the flat side of a cookie, then top with a second cookie, flat sides facing. Press gently to make the two cookies adhere. (The cookies can be stored in an airtight container for up to 4 days.) Just before serving, sift confectioners' sugar, if using, over the tops of the cookies.

NOTE: Dulce de leche can be purchased in cans or jars at Latino groceries and many supermarkets and specialty food stores. You can buy authentic Argentinean dulce de leche online from www.amigofoods.com. Leftover dulce de leche can be refrigerated in a covered container for up to 2 weeks. It is great stirred into hot tea instead of milk and sugar.

CHOCOLATE SANDWICH COOKIES WITH EARL GREY GANACHE ❧

MAKES ABOUT 2½ DOZEN COOKIES

For tea lovers who also have a passion for chocolate, these cookies will be heaven-sent. Rounds of chocolate sugar cookies are joined with Earl Grey tea ganache, which adds the citruslike taste and perfume of bergamot orange to the filling. Milk chocolate is used in the ganache, as bittersweet chocolate could overpower the tea. Rather than being rolled and cut out, the cookie dough here is formed into a log, refrigerated, and sliced into rounds, so allow time for the dough to chill. It goes without saying that Earl Grey is the perfect tea to serve with these treats.

CHOCOLATE SUGAR COOKIES

2 cups all-purpose flour

½ cup Dutch-processed cocoa power

½ teaspoon baking powder

½ teaspoon salt

1 cup (2 sticks) unsalted butter, at room temperature

½ cup granulated sugar

¼ cup packed light brown sugar

EARL GREY GANACHE

¾ cup heavy cream

1 tablespoon Earl Grey tea leaves

4 ounces milk chocolate, finely chopped

1. To make the cookies, sift the flour, cocoa, baking powder, and salt together. Cream the butter in a medium bowl with an electric mixer on high speed until the butter is creamy, about 1 minute. Gradually beat in the granulated and brown sugars until the mixture is light in color and texture, about 3 minutes. Gradually stir in the flour mixture to make a soft dough.

2. Divide the dough into thirds. Wrap each portion of dough in wax paper to make a log about 5½ inches long and 1½ inches in diameter. Twist the ends closed. Refrigerate until the dough is chilled and firm enough to cut and hold its shape, at least 2 hours and up to 2 days. (If the dough is chilled until it is very hard, let it stand to soften slightly for about 10 minutes before slicing, or the cookie slices could crack.)

3. Position a rack in the top third and center of the oven and preheat to 350°F. Line two large baking sheets with parchment paper.

4. Using a sharp, thin-bladed knife, cut the dough rolls into ¼-inch-thick rounds. Place about 1 inch apart on the baking sheets. Bake, switching the position of the baking sheets from top to bottom and front to back halfway through baking, until the edges of the cookies feel firm when lightly pressed, about 12 minutes. Let cool for 5 minutes on the baking sheets. Transfer to wire cake racks and let cool completely.

5. To make the ganache, bring the heavy cream to a simmer in a small saucepan over medium heat. Remove from the heat and stir in the tea. Let stand for 5 minutes. Strain the cream mixture through a wire sieve into a bowl, pressing hard on the tea. Return the strained cream to the saucepan and reheat to a simmer. Put the chocolate in a small heat-proof bowl. Add the hot cream mixture and let stand until the chocolate softens, about 3 minutes. Stir with a rubber or silicone spatula until the chocolate melts. Place the small bowl in a larger bowl of ice water and let stand, stirring and scraping the sides of the small bowl often with the spatula, until cooled and thickened to a spreadable consistency.

6. Transfer the ganache to a pastry bag fitted with a ½-inch fluted tip, such as Ateco #825. Pipe a rosette of ganache on the flat side of one cookie, and sandwich it with a second cookie, flat sides together. (Or omit the pastry bag and tip, and simply spread the cookie with about 2 teaspoons of the ganache.) Repeat with the remaining cookies. Let stand until the ganache sets, about 1 hour. (The cookies can be stored in an airtight container and refrigerated for up to 2 days. Let stand at room temperature for 30 minutes before serving.)

❧ MACARONS DE CITRON

Colorful *macarons* are a mainstay of Parisian tearooms and bakeries, and this pastel yellow lemon version is just the thing to nibble with a bracing black tea. Note that a French *macaron* (two smooth almond-based cookies sandwiched together with a tasty filling) is much different from an American macaroon. This cookie can be temperamental to make at home without a professional oven. After much experimentation, I have found the almond flour to be an important component; almonds ground in a food processor won't work. One other tip: Make the meringue base in a heatproof bowl, but not the bowl of a heavy-duty mixer, as the amount isn't sufficient for the whisk attachment to whip properly. If your *macarons* aren't picture-perfect, don't fret, as they will be highly edible anyway.

MACARONS

1 cup plus 3 tablespoons almond flour
(see Note)

1¼ cups confectioners' sugar

Grated zest of 1 lemon

3 large egg whites

⅓ cup plus 2 tablespoons granulated sugar

Yellow food coloring (optional)

LEMON BUTTERCREAM

1 large egg white

¼ cup granulated sugar

8 tablespoons (1 stick) unsalted butter,
at cool room temperature

Grated zest of 1 lemon

1 teaspoon fresh lemon juice

1. Line a large baking sheet with parchment paper. Process the almond flour and confectioners' sugar in a food processor fitted with the metal blade until the mixture is very fine, about 30 seconds. Add the lemon zest and pulse to combine.

2. Whisk the egg whites and granulated sugar together in a stainless-steel medium bowl that fits snugly over a medium saucepan of simmering water (the bottom of the bowl should not touch the water). Heat the egg white mixture over the water, whisking constantly, until it is hot and opaque white, and the sugar is dissolved (dip in a clean finger to check), about 2 minutes. Remove from the heat. Using a hand-held electric mixer set at high speed (or a balloon whisk), beat until the meringue forms stiff, shiny peaks. Add a tiny amount of yellow food coloring to heighten the color, if you wish.

3. In two additions, sprinkle the almond mixture over the meringue and fold it in. Do not overmix. Transfer the batter to a pastry bag fitted with a ½-inch plain pastry tip, such as Ateco #805. Pipe twenty-four 2-inch-diameter domes of the batter on the baking sheet, spacing the domes about 1 inch apart. Smooth the tips of the domes with a water-moistened finger, if necessary. Let the *macarons* stand at room temperature for 20 minutes to 2 hours before baking. (This dries the surfaces slightly and makes for a better-looking cookie.)

4. Position a rack in the center of the oven and preheat to 325°F.

5. Bake for 5 minutes. Place a wooden spoon in the oven door to keep it ajar. Continue baking until the *macarons* are risen and set (a *macaron* will move as a unit if you wiggle it lightly with a finger), about 12 minutes longer.

6. Let cool on the baking sheet for 5 minutes. Using a small metal spatula, transfer the *macarons* to a wire cake rack and let cool completely.

7. To make the buttercream, combine the egg white and granulated sugar in a heatproof medium bowl. Place the bowl over a saucepan of simmering water over medium heat. Whisk the mixture until it is hot and opaque white, and the sugar is dissolved (dip in your finger to check), about 1½ minutes. Remove from the heat and place on a wire cake rack (to improve the air circulation under the bowl and speed cooling). Beat with a hand-held electric mixer with clean beaters on high speed until the meringue is very stiff and cooled, about 5 minutes. One tablespoon at a time, beat in the butter. Beat in the lemon zest and juice. Beat until the buttercream is very light and fluffy, about 1 minute.

8. Using a small offset metal spatula or the back of a spoon, spread one flat side of a *macaron* with the filling, then sandwich it with a second *macaron*, flat sides facing. Let stand until the filling sets. (The cookies can be made up to 3 days ahead, stored in an airtight container at room temperature.)

LEMON CURD MACARONS: Substitute about ²/₃ cup store-bought lemon curd for the lemon buttercream.

NOTE: Almond flour (also called almond meal) is available at natural food stores and well-stocked groceries. Even though they are not marked as such, there are two varieties—ivory-colored (made from blanched almonds) and brown (ground from unskinned almonds). The texture and color of the former is lighter and makes a superior *macaron* batter. Unfortunately, it is also more expensive than the brown flour.

CHERRY AND CHOCOLATE RUGELACH ❧

MAKES 45 COOKIES

These culinary icons of Jewish cuisine seem to be made for conversation over a steaming pot of tea. The exceptional dough (the secret is whipped cream cheese) comes from my friends Jeff and Ali Nathan, who taught me almost everything I know about Jewish cooking. While the classic rugelach filling contains nuts and raisins, there are as many variations as there are cooks, and I am very partial to this chocolate and cherry version. You might want to serve these with a strong Caravan tea, using cherry preserves instead of sugar for sweetening in the Russian manner.

DOUGH

1 cup (2 sticks) unsalted butter, at room temperature

One 8-ounce container whipped cream cheese

2 tablespoons sugar

½ teaspoon vanilla extract

¼ teaspoon salt

2 cups all-purpose flour

FILLING

¾ cup finely chopped walnuts

½ cup mini chocolate chips

3 tablespoons sugar

½ teaspoon ground cinnamon

¾ cup cherry preserves, processed in a food processor or blender to mince the fruit

1. To make the dough, beat the butter and cream cheese in a large bowl with an electric mixer on high speed (a standing electric mixer works best) until smooth and creamy, about 1 minute. Beat in the sugar, vanilla, and salt. On low speed, gradually add the flour and mix just until combined.

2. Turn out the dough onto a lightly floured work surface and knead briefly just until smooth. Divide the dough into thirds. Shape each portion into a thick rectangle and wrap in plastic wrap. Refrigerate until chilled, at least 1 hour and up to 1 day.

3. To make the filling, mix the walnuts and chocolate chips together in a medium bowl.

4. Position racks in the center and top third of the oven and preheat to 350°F. Line two large baking sheets with parchment paper.

5. Mix the sugar and cinnamon together. Unwrap one portion of dough and place on a lightly floured work surface. Sprinkle the top lightly with flour, then roll out into a 14 x 6-inch rectangle. (If the dough cracks, let it stand at room temperature for 5 minutes to soften slightly, then try again.) Spread about ¼ cup of the preserves over the dough, leaving a ½-inch-wide border at all sides. Sprinkle with one-third of the walnut-chocolate mixture, then a generous tablespoon of the sugar-cinnamon mixture. Starting at the long end, roll up into a tight cylinder, and pinch the long seam closed. Using a sharp knife, cut crosswise into 15 pieces. Repeat with the remaining ingredients. Place the rugelach, cut sides down, 1 inch apart on the baking sheets.

6. Bake until lightly browned, switching the position of the sheets from top to bottom and front to back halfway through baking, about 25 minutes. Let cool on the baking sheets for 5 minutes. Transfer the rugelach to wire cake racks and cool completely. (The rugelach can be stored in an airtight container at room temperature for up to 5 days.)

CLASSIC RUGELACH: In the filling, substitute ½ cup dried currants for the chocolate chips and apricot or seedless raspberry preserves for the cherry preserves. Increase the cinnamon to 1½ teaspoons.

PEANUT BUTTER AND JELLY COOKIES ❧

MAKES ABOUT 2½ DOZEN COOKIES

A variation on thumbprint cookies, these little mouthfuls have become one of my favorite teatime nibbles. Of course, the combination of peanut butter and grape jelly is classic, but you can use your preferred preserves, jam, or jelly—strawberry or raspberry preserves are also wonderful. I can't think of a better cookie for a young girl's tea party.

½ cup smooth or crunchy peanut butter
(see Note)

8 tablespoons (1 stick) unsalted butter,
at room temperature

½ cup packed light brown sugar

1 large egg, beaten

1 teaspoon vanilla extract

1½ cups all-purpose flour

½ teaspoon fine sea salt

About ½ cup grape jelly or your
favorite preserves, jam, or jelly

1. Position racks in the center and upper third of the oven and preheat to 375°F. Line two large baking sheets with parchment paper.

2. Beat the peanut butter and butter together in a medium bowl with an electric mixer on medium speed until combined, about 1 minute. Gradually beat in the brown sugar and continue beating until the mixture is light in color and texture, about 2 minutes. Beat in the egg and vanilla. On low speed, add the flour and salt and mix just until the dough is smooth.

3. Using about 1 tablespoon of dough for each cookie, roll the dough into 1-inch balls. Place about 1 inch apart on the baking sheets. Bake until the dough looks set, about 5 minutes.

4. Remove the baking sheets from the oven. Using the end of a wooden spoon, poke a hole about ½ inch wide and ½ inch deep in the center of each ball of dough. The balls will crack slightly, but don't worry. Return the baking sheets to the oven, switching their positions from top to bottom and front to back. Continue baking until the cookies are beginning to brown, about 5 minutes more.

5. Meanwhile, stir the grape jelly well in a small bowl to smooth it out. Transfer the jelly to a 1-quart self-sealing plastic bag, and squeeze the jelly into one corner of the bag. Close the bag and snip off the jelly-filled corner of the bag to make a ¼-inch-wide opening.

6. Remove the baking sheets from the oven. Using the plastic bag, fill each hole with jelly. Return the baking sheets to the oven and bake until the cookies are golden brown, about 2 minutes longer. Let cool completely on the baking sheets.

NOTE: Use the standard hydrogenated peanut butter, as all-natural brands don't work well in this dough.

AUSTRIAN SANDWICH COOKIES

MAKES ABOUT 32 COOKIES

These sandwich cookies sport bull's-eye holes with preserves peeking through. They were a common component of my aunties' cookie trays (not that my aunties ever made anything common). Kids love to help sandwich the cookies together, and quickly learn to apply just enough pressure to adhere the halves without breaking them. For a picture-perfect finish, spoon a little extra preserves into each hole to completely fill the cookies. While I am not a big fan of fruit teas, I often serve an apricot- or raspberry-flavored tea that matches the preserves in the filling.

3 cups all-purpose flour

2 teaspoons baking powder

½ teaspoon salt

10 tablespoons (1¼ sticks) unsalted butter, at room temperature

1¼ cups granulated sugar

2 large eggs, beaten, at room temperature

Grated zest of ½ lemon

1 cup apricot or raspberry preserves

Confectioners' sugar for garnish

1. Sift the flour, baking powder, and salt together. Cream the butter in a medium bowl with an electric mixer set on high speed until smooth, about 1 minute. Gradually beat in the granulated sugar until the mixture is very light in color and texture, about 2 minutes. Gradually beat in the eggs, then the lemon zest. Gradually stir in the flour mixture to make a soft dough.

2. Divide the dough in half and shape each portion into a thick disk. Wrap each in plastic wrap or wax paper. Refrigerate until chilled and firm enough to roll out, at least 2 hours

and up to 1 day. (If the dough is very chilled and hard, let it stand at room temperature for 10 minutes to slightly soften before rolling out.)

3. Position racks in the top third and center of the oven and preheat the oven to 350°F. Line two large baking sheets with parchment paper.

4. Unwrap one portion of dough and place on a lightly floured work surface. Dust the top with flour and roll out ⅛ inch thick. Using a 2¼-inch-diameter cookie cutter, cut out rounds of dough and transfer them to a baking sheet, placing them 1 inch apart. Gather up the scraps and roll out until all of the dough has been used. Refrigerate while cutting out the other portion of dough. Using a 1-inch-diameter cookie cutter, cut out a hole from the center of each round on the second baking sheet. Because the cookies with the holes will bake more quickly than the whole ones, keep the cookies on separate baking sheets. If you wish, gather up scraps from the holes and roll them out to make a few more cookies.

5. Bake, switching the position of the baking sheets from top to bottom and front to back halfway through baking, until the edges of the cookies are light golden brown, about 12 minutes for the perforated cookies and 15 minutes for the whole ones.

6. Let cool on the baking sheets for 5 minutes. Transfer to wire cake racks and let cool completely.

7. Heat the preserves in a small saucepan until boiling. Rub through a wire sieve set over a bowl, discarding the solids in the sieve. Spread about 1 teaspoon of the warm preserves over each whole (uncut) cookie. Top each with a perforated cookie and press gently to make them adhere. If desired, use a small demitasse spoon to completely fill the holes with the remaining preserves. Let cool until the preserves are set. (The cookies can be stored in an airtight container for up to 4 days.) Just before serving, sift confectioners' sugar over the tops of the cookies.

CANDIED WALNUT TASSIES

In China, candied walnuts, often seasoned with five-spice powder (a fragrant blend of cinnamon, fennel, star anise, cloves, and Sichuan peppercorns used in Asian cooking), are a favorite nibble to enjoy with tea. They've been transformed into the filling for these tender miniature tarts with a cream cheese crust and a pecan pie–like filling. You will need two 12-cup miniature muffin pans (each cup measuring 1⅞ inches across the top and ⅞ inch deep), preferably nonstick, to make these. For a quick way to press the dough into the muffin cups, invest in a wooden tart tamper (available at www.amazon.com and www.fantes.com), which is a very useful and inexpensive tool. I serve these with a strong black Chinese tea, such as Keemun, which helps balance the cookies' sweetness.

CRUST

1 cup all-purpose flour

Pinch of salt

7 tablespoons unsalted butter, cut into tablespoons, at room temperature

3 ounces cream cheese, cut into tablespoons, at room temperature

Nonstick vegetable oil spray (optional)

FILLING

¾ cup packed light brown sugar

1 large egg, at room temperature

1 tablespoon unsalted butter, melted

1 tablespoon light corn syrup or golden syrup

¾ teaspoon Asian five-spice powder

Pinch of salt

1 cup finely chopped walnuts

1. To make the crust, combine the flour and salt in a food processor fitted with the metal chopping blade and pulse to combine. Add the room-temperature butter and cream cheese and pulse about 15 times, until the mixture begins to clump together. Gather up the dough and shape into a thick disk. Wrap in plastic wrap and refrigerate until chilled and easy to handle, 1 to 2 hours.

2. Position a rack in the center of the oven and preheat to 350°F. Have ready two 12-cup miniature muffin pans (each cup measuring 1⅞ inches across the top and ⅞ inch deep), preferably nonstick. If the pans are not nonstick, spray them with vegetable oil.

3. Divide the dough into 24 equal pieces. One at a time, place a piece of dough in a muffin cup and use your fingers to press it firmly and evenly up the sides to make a pastry shell. (A wooden tart tamper can help the job go quickly.) Freeze for 5 minutes.

4. To make the filling, whisk the brown sugar, egg, melted butter, corn syrup, five-spice powder, and salt together in a medium bowl. Add the walnuts and stir well. Fill the muffin cups with the filling (a demitasse spoon is the perfect size for transferring the filling to the cups).

5. Bake until the crust is golden brown and the filling feels set when pressed with your fingers, about 30 minutes. Let the tassies cool in the pans on wire cake racks for 10 minutes. Carefully remove them from the pans (you may need to use the tip of a knife to help coax them free). Transfer to wire cake racks to cool completely. (The cookies can be stored in an airtight container, with the layers separated by wax or parchment paper, at room temperature for up to 3 days.)

SUGAR COOKIE TEAPOTS

For a very special tea party, serve these lovely decorated sugar cookies, baked in the shape of teapots (or teacups). Yes, you can simply bake the cookies and serve them *au naturel*, but they can be successfully iced and decorated even by those of us who aren't particularly artistic. These can be as plain or fancy as you wish, and you may find it more time-efficient to bake the cookies a day or two before icing them at your leisure. To paint patterns onto the cookies, buy new children's paint brushes and save the brushes for the next time you want decorated cookies. For tea party–inspired cookie cutters, go to www.thecookiecuttershop.com.

SUGAR COOKIES

3 cups all-purpose flour

1 cup granulated sugar

1½ teaspoons baking powder

½ teaspoon salt

1 cup (2 sticks) cold unsalted butter, cut into tablespoons

¼ cup heavy cream

1 large egg plus 1 large egg yolk

1½ teaspoons vanilla extract

....

Royal Icing (page 127)

Food coloring paste

Dragées for decorating

1. To make the cookies, sift the flour, sugar, baking powder, and salt together into a large bowl. Add the butter. Using an electric mixer set at low speed, cut the butter into the flour until the mixture resembles coarse bread crumbs, about 2 minutes.

2. Mix the cream, whole egg, egg yolk, and vanilla together well. Add to the flour mixture and stir to form a soft dough. Gather the dough together and divide into two thick disks. Wrap each disk in plastic wrap. Refrigerate until chilled, at least 2 hours and up to 24 hours.

3. Position racks in the center and top third of the oven and preheat to 350°F. Line two large baking sheets with parchment paper.

4. To roll out the cookies, work with one disk at a time. Remove the dough from the refrigerator and let stand at room temperature until malleable enough to roll out without cracking, about 5 minutes. (If the dough has been chilled more than 2 hours, let stand a few more minutes.) Unwrap the dough and place on a lightly floured work surface. Lightly sprinkle the top of the dough with flour. Roll out the dough to slightly more than ⅛ inch thick. (A silicone rolling pin works best for this somewhat sticky dough.) As you roll out the dough, it will become easier to work with, and tiny cracks on the surface will disappear. Occasionally run a long knife or metal offset spatula under the dough to be sure it isn't sticking, and dust more flour under the dough if needed.

5. Using teapot or teacup cookie cutters, cut out the cookies and transfer to the baking sheets, placing the cookies 1 inch apart. Gently knead the scraps together and form into another disk. Wrap and freeze for 5 minutes before rolling out to cut out more cookies. In the meantime, work with the other disk of dough.

6. Bake, switching the position of the cookie sheets from top to bottom and front to back halfway through baking, just until the edges of the cookies are turning brown, about 10 minutes. Do not overbake. Let cool on the cookie sheets for 10 minutes. Transfer to wire racks and let cool completely. (The plain cookies without icing can be stored in an airtight container at room temperature for up to 2 days or frozen for up to 1 month. Defrost before using.)

7. Transfer about 1½ cups of royal icing to a mixing bowl. Tightly cover the remaining icing. Whisk in enough water to give the icing the consistency of thick heavy cream. Tint the icing to your desired color. Using a small metal offset spatula, ice the top of each cookie, smoothing the edges of the cookie with the spatula to let any excess icing drip back into the bowl. While the icing is still wet, place a dragée in the top of the teapot to simulate the lid handle. Place the cookies on wire cake racks and let the icing dry completely, at least 1 hour.

8. If you wish to make a pattern on the cookies, divide the remaining icing into the desired number of colors in small bowls. Tint each bowl of icing to the desired color. Thin each bowl of icing to the consistency of paint. Using a thin paintbrush, decorate the dried icing surfaces of the cookies as desired. Let dry completely. (The iced cookies can be stored in airtight containers at room temperature for up to 5 days.)

ROYAL ICING ❧

Royal icing will give your cookies a glossy professional-looking sheen. It was originally made with raw egg whites, but these days the chance of salmonella in uncooked eggs makes an icing that will be standing for long periods at room temperature risky. Luckily, there are many egg white products where processing has killed any trace of salmonella. This recipe uses dried egg white powder, but see the note for alternatives.

1 pound (3¾ cups)
confectioners' sugar, sifted

2 tablespoons dried egg white powder
(see Note)

Combine the confectioners' sugar, egg white powder, and 6 tablespoons water in the bowl of a heavy-duty standing mixer fitted with the paddle attachment. Mix on low speed until combined. Increase the speed to high and beat, scraping down the sides of the bowl often, until very stiff and shiny, about 4 minutes. Use immediately.

NOTE: Dried egg white powder is available in the bakery supply section at many grocery stores. You can substitute meringue powder, available at baking supply stores and hobby shops. Or use pasteurized egg whites, found in the refrigerated section of the supermarket, which do not have to be reconstituted. Substitute ¼ cup plus 2 tablespoons pasteurized egg whites for the dried egg whites and water.

TEAROOM TREATS

As tea is served in every corner of the world, the venue and menu will change according to the culture. Each of these cookies is a reminder of a specific place where tea is served, from the elegant salons of Europe to the quiet Japanese teahouses and the more boisterous tearooms of China. I have been sure to include a version of onc of the most famous pairings of food and tea—Proust's madeleines dipped in lime blossom tea.

ORANGE AND PINE NUT BISCOTTI

There are basically two kinds of biscotti in the world, those made with butter or oil, and those made without. Frankly, the latter are more authentically Italian, and especially crunchy. These orange and pine nut biscotti are Americanized, but they do not suffer from the addition of butter. Try them dipped in any citrus-flavored or Earl Grey tea.

2¼ cups all-purpose flour

1 teaspoon baking powder

¼ teaspoon salt

8 tablespoons (1 stick) unsalted butter, at room temperature

1 cup sugar

Grated zest of 1 orange

2 large eggs, beaten, at room temperature

1 teaspoon vanilla extract

1 cup pine nuts

1. Position racks in the center and top third of the oven and preheat to 325°F.

2. Sift the flour, baking powder, and salt together. Beat the butter, sugar, and orange zest together in a medium bowl with an electric mixer on high speed until light in color and texture, about 3 minutes. Do not overmix. Gradually beat in the eggs, then the vanilla. Gradually stir in the flour mixture to make a stiff dough. Stir in the pine nuts.

3. Divide the dough in half. Using lightly floured hands on a floured work surface, form the dough into two 10 x 2-inch rectangular logs—make the ends flat, not pointed. Transfer the logs to a baking sheet, placing them at least 2 inches apart. Bake on the

center rack of the oven until the logs are set and golden brown, about 30 minutes. Remove from the oven and let cool on the baking sheet for 20 minutes.

4. Using a serrated knife and a sawing motion, carefully cut the logs into diagonal slices about ½ inch wide. Place the slices on ungreased baking sheets. Bake until the undersides of the biscotti are lightly browned, about 8 minutes. Turn the biscotti over. Switch the position of the baking sheets from top to bottom and front to back. Continue baking until lightly browned on the other side, about 8 minutes longer. Let cool completely on the baking sheets. (The biscotti can be stored in an airtight container for up to 1 week.)

GREEN TEA CUSTARD TARTLETS

Custard tartlets are almost always offered as part of the Chinese and Japanese tea service. Flavored and colored with green matcha tea, these tartlets mix old and new as well as a combination of Asian and Western cuisines. I served these as the sweet component of a dim sum menu (the dumplings courtesy of my local Chinese restaurant), and they were a huge hit. Serve them with your favorite green tea— gunpowder would be my personal choice.

CREAM CHEESE CRUST

1 cup all-purpose flour

Pinch of salt

7 tablespoons unsalted butter, cut into tablespoons, at room temperature

3 ounces cream cheese, cut into tablespoons, at room temperature

Nonstick vegetable oil spray (optional)

FILLING

3 large egg yolks

⅓ cup sugar

1 teaspoon matcha (powdered green tea)

1 cup whole milk, heated

1. To make the crust, combine the flour and salt in a food processor fitted with the metal chopping blade and pulse to combine. Add the butter and cream cheese and pulse about 15 times, until the mixture begins to clump together. Gather up the dough and shape into a thick disk. Wrap in plastic wrap and refrigerate until chilled and easy to handle, 1 to 2 hours.

2. Position a rack in the center of the oven and preheat to 350°F. Have ready two 12-cup miniature muffin pans (each cup measuring 1⅞ inches across the top and ⅞ inch deep), preferably nonstick. If the pans are not nonstick, spray them with vegetable oil.

3. Divide the dough into 24 equal pieces. One at a time, place a piece of dough in a muffin cup, and use your fingers to press it firmly and evenly up the sides to make a pastry shell. (A wooden tart tamper can help the job go quickly.) Freeze for 5 minutes.

4. To make the filling, whisk the yolks, sugar, and matcha together in a medium bowl. Gradually whisk in the milk—the mixture will be very foamy. Pour into a glass measuring cup. Let stand for a few minutes, then skim off the foam from the top of the milk mixture. Place the miniature muffin pans on a large baking sheet. Divide the milk mixture evenly among the pastry shells.

5. Bake until the edges of the tartlets are golden brown and the filling is set (a knife inserted in the center will come out almost clean), 30 to 35 minutes. Let the tartlets cool in the pans on wire cake racks for 10 minutes. Carefully remove them from the muffin pans (you may need to use the tip of a knife to help coax them from the pans). Transfer to a wire cake rack to cool completely. (The cookies can be stored in an airtight container, with the layers separated by wax or parchment paper, in the refrigerator for up to 3 days. Let stand at room temperature for 30 minutes before serving.)

LEMON TEA "CAKES"

The British tea tradition includes tea "cakes," which are actually cookies. Like shortbread, another British teatime essential, these have just a few ingredients, allowing the flavor of the tea to take center stage. This recipe comes from my cousin, Judy Knecht, who makes it often for just about any kind of a social gathering from church meetings to ladies' luncheons.

2 lemons	1¼ cups confectioners' sugar, divided
1 cup (2 sticks) unsalted butter, at room temperature	3 tablespoons fresh lemon juice
	2¼ cups all-purpose flour

1. Using a rasp-style zester, grate the zest from the lemons. Juice the lemons and reserve the 3 tablespoons.

2. Mix the butter and ½ cup of the confectioners' sugar together in a medium bowl with an electric mixer on low speed just until combined. Increase the speed to high and beat until the mixture is light in color and texture, about 3 minutes. Beat in the lemon juice and half of the zest. Stir in the flour and mix just until the dough is combined. Cover and refrigerate until chilled and firm enough to handle, at least 1 hour and up to 4 hours.

3. Position a rack in the top third and center of the oven and preheat to 350°F. Line two large baking sheets with parchment paper.

4. Using a scant tablespoon for each cookie, roll the dough into 1-inch balls and place 2 inches apart on the baking sheets. Bake, switching the position of the baking sheets

from top to bottom and front to back halfway through baking, until the cookies are light golden brown on the bottom, about 16 minutes. Let cool on the sheets for 5 minutes.

5. Combine the remaining ¾ cup sugar and the zest in a small bowl, working them together with your fingertips. One at a time, roll the warm cookies in the lemon sugar to coat, and transfer to another baking sheet to cool completely. Reserve the remaining lemon sugar. (The cookies and lemon sugar can be made up to 1 day ahead, stored at room temperature in separate airtight containers.) Just before serving, roll the cookies again in the remaining lemon sugar.

❦ LIME MADELEINES

I wonder how many people have been inspired to make madeleines by reading Proust's evocation of his dipping one of the cakelike cookies into a cup of lime blossom tea. Madeleines are made from the most basic of pastry ingredients, yet some bakers find them tricky, so I've included many tips in my recipe.

Softened unsalted butter for the pans

8 tablespoons (1 stick) unsalted butter, cut into tablespoons

Grated zest of 1 lime

½ teaspoon vanilla extract

3 large eggs, at room temperature

⅔ cup sugar

⅔ cup all-purpose flour

¼ teaspoon salt

1. Using a pastry brush, generously butter the molds in two madeleine pans, being sure to get into the grooves. Do not flour the pans. Place the pans in the freezer to chill while making the batter.

2. Melt the butter in a small, heavy-bottomed saucepan over medium heat, and let boil until the milk solids in the bottom of the pan turn light brown, 2 to 3 minutes. Remove from the heat and let stand for 1 minute. Skim the foam from the top of the butter. Carefully pour the browned butter into a medium bowl, leaving the browned milk solids behind in the saucepan. Let stand until tepid, about 15 minutes. Add the lime zest and vanilla.

3. Crack the eggs into a heatproof medium bowl and place in a larger bowl of hot tap water. With a clean finger stir the eggs until they lose their chill and are heated until

lukewarm. Add the sugar. Beat with an electric mixer on high speed until the mixture is tripled in volume and very pale yellow, about 4 minutes.

4. Whisk the flour and salt together. In two additions, sift over the egg mixture and fold it in with a large balloon whisk or a rubber spatula. Transfer about one-fourth of the batter to the butter-vanilla mixture and whisk together to combine. Return this mixture to the batter and fold it in. Cover the bowl with plastic wrap and refrigerate until the batter is chilled, at least 1 hour and up to 2 hours.

5. Position a rack in the center of the oven and preheat to 375°F. Spoon equal amounts of the batter into the chilled molds, filling them about two-thirds full. Do not overfill the molds. The mounds of chilled batter will help the madeleines bake with their characteristic hump, so do not smooth the batter.

6. Bake until the madeleines are golden brown and begin to shrink from the sides of the molds, about 15 minutes. Let cool in the pans for 5 minutes. Using the dull tip of a dinner knife, gently loosen each madeleine from its mold. Invert each pan and rap it on the work surface to release the madeleines. Transfer to a wire cake rack and let cool completely. (The madeleines can be stored in an airtight container at room temperature for up to 2 days.)

LAVENDER MADELEINES: These perfumed madeleines are for your tea guests with the most sophisticated palates. Omit the lime zest. Grind 1 teaspoon dried lavender in a mortar and pestle or in a spice grinder into a coarse powder. (Be sure to use edible dried lavender, available at spice stores and many supermarkets, and not sprayed lavender intended for potpourri.) Add the lavender to the skimmed browned butter in the bowl and let stand for 20 minutes.

MADELEINE PANS

Madeleine pans have shell-shaped indentations and are made of aluminum, tin, or plain or black steel. While there are nonstick pans, most are uncoated, making the baked cookies difficult to remove. A generous brushing of well-softened butter (rather than a dusting of flour) helps solve this problem, and adds to the browning of the madeleines as well. The black steel pans absorb the oven heat more readily than the shiny metal ones. Because of this, madeleines baked in black pans bake quickly, so watch them carefully to avoid burning.

CURRANT CREAM SCONES

Scones, being cut from dough, are not-too-distant relatives of cookies, and, of course, they are forever associated with tea. Slather these flaky, buttery scones with clotted cream or butter and a good jam, and you will be transported to the British Isles. Take care when rerolling the scraps: Just gather up the bits of dough and press them gently together, as overhandling will lead to tough scones.

2 cups all-purpose flour

2 tablespoons sugar

1 tablespoon baking powder

¼ teaspoon salt

8 tablespoons (1 stick) unsalted butter, cut into ½-inch cubes, chilled

½ cup dried currants

1 large egg yolk

Scant 1 cup heavy cream, as needed, plus more for glazing the scones

1. Position a rack in the center of the oven and preheat to 400°F. Line a large baking sheet with parchment paper.

2. Sift the flour, sugar, baking powder, and salt together. Add the butter and mix to separate the butter cubes and coat them with flour. Using a pastry blender, cut the cubes into the flour mixture until the mixture resembles coarse bread crumbs with pea-size pieces of butter. Do not cut until the mixture is evenly crumbly—the larger pieces of butter will help make the scones flaky. Add the currants.

3. Put the yolk in a 1- or 2-cup glass measuring cup and add enough heavy cream to measure 1 cup and beat together with a fork to combine. Stirring the flour mixture with a large fork, add the cream mixture and mix just until a soft, tacky dough forms.

4. Turn the dough out onto a lightly floured surface. Using lightly floured hands, pat the dough into a ¾-inch-thick round. Using a 2¼-inch-diameter biscuit cutter, cut out the scones and transfer to the baking sheet. Gather up the scraps, pat out again, and cut the remaining scones. Brush the tops lightly with cream.

5. Bake until the scones are golden brown, 18 to 20 minutes. Cool slightly, then serve warm or cool to room temperature. (The scones are best the day they are made. Leftovers can be wrapped airtight and frozen for up to 1 month. Defrost, split, and toast the scones before serving warm.)

CLASSIC TRIANGULAR SCONES: Scones are named for the Stone of Scone, a triangular rock formation that was the traditional throne of the kings of Scotland. Cutting the dough in the classic wedge shape sidesteps the problem of rerolling the scraps that occur when the scones are cut into rounds. Pat out the dough into an 8-inch round about ¾ inch thick. Cut into 8 equal wedges. Place 1 inch apart on the baking sheet, brush with cream, and bake as directed above.

❧ PISTACHIO MERINGUES

MAKES ABOUT 2½ DOZEN COOKIES

Proust had his madeleines, but I have my meringues. During my first trip to Paris, every pastry shop held a new discovery. I remember the first time I experienced these cookies, shatteringly crisp on the outside, but creamy within, dotted with pistachios, at the premier Parisian tea shop, Mariage Frères. I brought back a bottle of pistachio extract with me so I could re-create the meringues at home. (You can find the extract online at www.amazon.com and www.jacksonvillemercantile.com.) Don't make these during humid or rainy weather, and be sure to allow plenty of time for them to bake slowly.

4 large egg whites, at room temperature

2¼ cups plus 1 tablespoon confectioners' sugar, divided

Green food coloring gel (optional)

¾ teaspoon pistachio or almond extract

½ cup (2 ounces) shelled pistachios

1. Position racks in the center and top third of the oven and preheat to 200°F. Line two large baking sheets with parchment paper.

2. Whip the egg whites in a medium bowl with an electric mixer at medium speed until they are foamy. Increase the speed to high and add 2¼ cups of the confectioners' sugar, a tablespoon at a time. Continue beating until the mixture forms stiff, shiny peaks. Tint the meringue pale green with the food coloring, if using. Beat in the pistachio extract.

3. Process the pistachios and the remaining 1 tablespoon confectioners' sugar in a food processor until very finely chopped. Fold into the egg white mixture.

4. Transfer the mixture to a pastry bag fitted with a ½-inch-diameter open star tip, such as Ateco #825. Pipe rosettes of the mixture, about 1 inch wide and 1 inch high, onto the baking sheets, spacing them about 1½ inches apart.

5. Bake, switching the position of the baking sheets from top to bottom and front to back halfway through baking, until the meringues are crisp and can be easily lifted from the baking sheets, about 2½ hours. Turn off the oven and prop the door ajar with a wooden spoon. Let the cookies cool on their sheets in the oven for at least 6 hours or overnight.

6. Remove from the baking sheets and serve. (The meringues can be stored in an airtight container for up to 5 days.)

SESAME BALLS ✛

These Asian-style cookies complement many teas, especially the hot Gingered Green Tea on page 31. For a dramatic look, substitute black sesame seeds (available at Asian and Indian markets) for the standard white seeds.

2½ cups all-purpose flour	2 large egg yolks
1½ teaspoons baking powder	¼ cup whole milk
12 tablespoons (1½ sticks) unsalted butter, at room temperature	½ teaspoon almond extract
1 cup sugar	½ cup hulled sesame seeds

1. Position a rack in the top third and center of the oven and preheat to 350°F. Line two large baking sheets with parchment paper.

2. Sift together the flour and baking powder. Mix the butter in a medium bowl with an electric mixer on high speed until creamy, about 1 minute. Gradually beat in the sugar until the mixture is light in color and texture, about 2 minutes. One at a time, beat in the yolks, then the milk and almond extract. Stir in the flour mixture until the dough is combined. Cover and refrigerate until chilled and firm enough to handle, at least 1 hour and up to 4 hours.

3. Using a scant tablespoon for each cookie, shape the dough into 1-inch balls. Roll in the sesame seeds to coat. Place 2 inches apart on the baking sheets. Bake, switching the position of the baking sheets from top to bottom and front to back halfway through baking, until the cookies are light golden brown on the bottom, about 15 minutes.

4. Let cool on the sheets for 5 minutes. Transfer to wire cake racks and cool completely. (The cookies can be made up to 5 days ahead, stored in airtight containers at room temperature.)

BROWN SUGAR SHORTBREAD

Shortbread—full of buttery flavor and a crumbly melt-in-your-mouth texture that few other cookies can deliver—is another item that must be included in most teatime menus. Brown sugar gives these a hint of molasses. For truly extraordinary results, instead of standard brown sugar, use muscovado sugar, which is made by a centuries-old process and has a deeper flavor.

1 cup (2 sticks) unsalted butter, at room temperature

½ cup packed light brown or muscovado sugar

1⅔ cups all-purpose flour

⅓ cup cornstarch

Pinch of salt

1. Position a rack in the center of the oven and preheat to 350°F. Lightly butter a 9- to 9½-inch springform pan.

2. Beat the butter in a medium bowl with an electric mixer set at high speed until smooth, about 1 minute. Add the sugar and beat until the mixture is light in color and texture, about 2 minutes. Using a wooden spoon, stir in the flour, cornstarch, and salt. Press the dough evenly into the pan. Using the tines of a fork, press around the perimeter of the dough. Prick the dough, reaching down to the bottom of the pan, into 10 equal wedges.

3. Bake until lightly browned, about 30 minutes. Cool completely in the pan. Remove the sides of the pan. Cut the shortbread into wedges, following the perforations in the dough. (The shortbread can be stored in an airtight container for up to 5 days.)

SOURCES

*There are countless places to buy tea and bakery supplies
online or by mail order. Here is a selective list of places
that I have personally done business with, and highly
recommend.*

ADMARI TEA
202 Franklin Avenue
Midland Park, NJ 07432
(201) 301-2801
www.admaritea.com

I love this store, touting (and delivering) personal
service and the very best loose-leaf teas both in the
charming little shop and online. Adrienne Etkin
travels around the world to find extraordinary
offerings. She also caters delicious tea parties.

AMAZON
www.amazon.com

The kitchen store at this online giant keeps getting
better and better. Check here for such formerly hard-
to-find items as pistachio extract, wooden tartlet
tampers, and flat parchment paper.

BOBA TEA DIRECT
9674 E. Arapahoe Road, #155
Greenwood Village, CO 80112
www.bobateadirect.com

There are many online stores to buy pearl
tapioca, wide straws, and other supplies for bubble
(boba) tea, but this one has an especially large
selection and sells in amounts manageable for the
home cook.

CHA MA GU DAO
212 Glenridge Avenue
Montclair, NJ 07042
(973) 746-0975
www.southsilkroad.com

A shop in the austere Asian style with an amazingly
diverse menu of hundreds of teas, Cha Ma Gu
Dao also sells their fine loose-leaf tea and teawares
online.

THE COOKIE CUTTER SHOP
3021 140th Street NW
Marysville, WA 98271
(360) 652-3295
www.thecookiecuttershop.com

The place to find charming and well-made cookie cutters, including teacups, teapots, and other kitchen-inspired shapes.

HARNEY AND SONS FINE TEAS
P.O. Box 665
Salisbury, CT 06068
(888) 427-6398
www.harney.com

Michael Harney sells a large variety of world-class tea for every taste in beautifully packaged canisters. Their silken sachets make believers out of tea-bag haters. If you are in the Berkshire Mountains, try their tasting room and restaurant in Millerton, New York.

PASTRY SAMPLER
Beach Cuisine, Inc.
1672 Main Street, Ste. E, #159
Ramona, CA 92065
(760) 440-9171
www.pastrysampler.com

One-stop shopping for all professional-quality baking supplies, this online store is where you'll find a wide assortment of pastry tips.

SUR LA TABLE
P.O. Box 840
Brownsburg, IN 46112
(800) 243-0852
www.surlatable.com

With more than seventy well-stocked stores nationwide, and a great online shop, you are likely to find what you are looking for at this top-notch kitchenware supplier.

T SALON
134 W. 26th Street, Fourth Floor
New York, NY 10001
(212) 358-0506
www.tsalon.com

T Salon has two wonderful shops, one in the Chelsea Market complex in Manhattan and the other on Melrose Avenue in Los Angeles. But the owner, Miriam Novalle, also has a fine online shop with such features as a "Tea of the Month Club" and samplers.

WILLIAMS-SONOMA
3250 Van Ness Avenue
San Francisco, CA 94109
(877) 812-6235
www.williams-sonoma.com

The kitchenware and tabletop giant remains a reliable place to buy top-of-the-line baking supplies from half-sheet pans to food coloring.

INDEX